# *International* ALCOHOL DRUG RESOURCE GUIDE

## *Free Alternative Recovery Programs* **On***Line and* **Off**

Plus How Not to Die in a Rehab

Steve Murray

International Alcohol Drug Resource Guide Free Alternative Recovery Programs OnLine and Off plus How Not to Die in a Rehab

ISBN 9780990446859

Library of Congress Control Number: 2018914346

by
Steve Murray

Published by
SPM  New York - London

First E Published April 2019

Includes references and index.
1. Drug Addiction 2. Alcohol Recovery 3. Alcoholism
4. Substance Abuse 5. Drug Recovery
Cover design: Sehee Han
Type design, production: Six Penny Graphics
Editor: Dr. Toni Briegel

# DISCLAIMER

The authors of this book do not dispense medical advice or prescribe the use of any method, technique and/or recovery program as a form of treatment for alcohol and/or drug addiction. The intent of the book is only to offer information to help inform you of addiction recovery options available. In the event you use any of the information in this book for yourself, or others, the authors and the publisher assume no responsibility for your actions or outcome of your actions.

Before starting any program, method or technique as described in the book, consult professional medical advice first.

All matters regarding your health require medical supervision. Neither the authors nor the publisher shall be liable or responsible for any loss or damage allegedly arising from any information in this book.

## Also by Steve Murray

This book is dedicated to Steven Paul Murray, Jr.

# CONTENTS

## Free Web Site Recovery Programs

## Free Moderate Drinking Programs

## Vitamin Protocol Programs

## Drug Protocol Programs

## Alcoholics Anonymous

## Resource Guide Two

# NOTE TO THE READER

All the previous books I have written have been self-help, spiritual books on healing the mental, emotional, physical, and spiritual body. This book, although a little detour on what I usually write in content, I do consider to be in my genre. It is a genuine self-help book and does give options and help on self-healing on all levels.

A few issues I want to clarify in case the reader gets the information misconstrued. By no means is this Guide a denunciation of all Rehabs and Alcoholic Anonymous (AA).

I would summarize (and hope) that most Rehabs do have the wellbeing of their patients at heart, and their employees are compassionate and trained. Unfortunately, there are some I label Toxic Rehabs and the Survivor calls bad apples. These Toxic Rehabs you need to be aware of, and these are the ones I write about. The remaining Rehabs, which I call the Good Guys, will embrace what I write because they have nothing to hide from their patients.

Alcoholics Anonymous is a great organization. Its recovery program has worked for thousands and thousands of people with addictions throughout the years. The challenge is, as I mention in the Guide, statistics show that AA is successful for maybe 5% to 10% of the people who use the program. The Guide gives alternative recovery programs for healing to the 90% to 95% of people AA unfortunately does not work for. It is as simple and equitable as that.

*Steve Murray*
vegasspiritualist@gmail.com
www.soberhelpbook.com
www.healingreiki.com

# CHAPTER ONE

# ORIGINS

I was visited by a good friend I had not seen for a while. He insisted on telling me his life-threating experience that occurred during his stay in an Alcohol and Drug Rehab. The story included the heavy-handed and intimidating tactics the Rehab used after he was discharged. He was adamant that I listen. The two-part saga seemed incredible and implausible. My first reaction was what most people would think. What? Rehabs are the addict's friend and savior and they are there to help. They're the Good Guys. So, how can his story have any merit?

The purpose of his visit was to cajole me into writing a book that warns people about the possible dangers of Rehabs based on his experiences during and after his own Rehab stint—a self-help book for addicts and their families to prevent them from having the same life-threating experiences.

After hearing his story, I told him "Leave your paperwork, will be in touch…" at the same time thinking, I'm not going to write such a book for a few compelling reasons. The content seemed out of my wheel house. No time for it. Working on one book and had one stacked right behind it. Didn't think there was need for such a book. Since he was a really good friend, I resigned myself to following through with a little research regarding his allegations and story.

He left medical paperwork from his four-day stay in Rehab. This was soon given to a seasoned registered nurse with 30 years' experience to decipher the medical mumbo jumbo to confirm his story. Documents were also left from the legal battle he had with the Rehab after his departure from their facility. These documents were presented to my personal attorney for his review and interpretation.

**Toxic Rehabs**

In the meantime, I started doing some light research on Alcohol Drug Rehabs in the USA. The research uncovered some problems within the Rehab Industry that could impact negatively or deny Rehab patients from having a successful recovery from their addiction(s). To compound that, some problems could cause Rehab patients (and their families) to suffer physically, emotionally and financially.

The initial findings intrigued and baffled me. This prompted more in-depth research. The end results were stunning! The Rehab industry in the United States is a non-fully regulated $35 billion dollar a year industry. Rehabs had not just a few problems as first discovered, but a myriad of problems. All caused by not being fully regulated. Rehabs had the potential of harming their patients on all levels. I decided to labeled these Rehabs, Toxic Rehabs.

By not having fully-trained medical employees, patients can die or be harmed because of negligence and incompetence in a Toxic Rehab. Toxic Rehabs have recovery treatment programs that do not work for many patients. To add insult to injury, many charge exorbitant fees for these programs. These are not only the problems at Toxic Rehabs. Specific concerns will be addressed and explained in Guide Two, "How Not to Die in Rehab."

## Complaints

On a hunch, I started googling Rehabs in large cities. I used search words such as "complaints rehabs." Each city googled had the same sad results, brutal complaints and reviews from previous patients about their terrible experiences in the local Rehabs. Warnings for prospective patients were also in the complaints. Their comments most likely were just the tip of the iceberg. It is a good assumption that hundreds of people in each city had not spoken out on social media about their terrible Rehab experiences.

I was appalled. How could any health industry with a public persona of helping people with addictions survive, let alone thrive with consumer complaints like this? Answers were needed. Wanting to find out if Rehab industry problems existed in other countries, Canada, the United Kingdom, and Australia were researched, to name a few. Yes, they did! Most countries have the same, if not similar, problematic issues with the Rehab Industry. This was an international phenomenon. My friend was correct. This is a book that needed to be written.

## The Nurse

The nurse said the paperwork she reviewed was sloppy, unprofessional, and the worst she had ever seen. After going over my friend's allegations about his stay in the Rehab, I asked, "Does the medical paperwork you reviewed substantiate what he says?" "Yes, and I am of the opinion your friend is very lucky to be alive from his experience with the Rehab. He could have died." Okay, the first part of my friend's story is holding up. And to give credibility to my friend's story, the nurse signed an affidavit[1] of her interpretation of the medical records.

## The Attorney

Soon after I met with my attorney. He stated the lawsuit instigated against my friend was a typical Strategic Lawsuit Against

---

1    Her affidavit is at the end of the Resource Guide.

Public Participation (SLAPP)[2], which basically is used to intimate a person and shut them up. Let me stop here and explain. Yes, my friend was sued by the Rehab. He claimed it was to shut him up about what happened and make him go away. The second part of my friend's story has held up. Credibility for both parts of his story has been established.

The attorney further elaborated, "The SLAPP tactic has been successfully used in the past by big business with deep pockets to cover up and keep their mistakes hidden from the public. It works because it is intimidating, stressful, creates fear, and drains the time and finances of the person who is on the receiving end of the lawsuit. Then to compound matters, an attorney needs to be hired to properly answer and defend the suit. When hiring an attorney, you can be talking $50,000 plus, depending on how hard the entity that sues you wants you to suffer financially before you throw in the towel. Lawsuits are not for the faint-hearted." I thanked him for his time.

My friend fought back, countersuing the Rehab despite the obstacles the attorney mentioned. That took a lot of courage and fortitude, not to mention the financial resources. Ultimately the law suit was settled in his favor. It was a complete struggle to victory.

---

2   A Strategic Lawsuit Against Public Participation (SLAPP) is a suit in which the plaintiff sues an organization or person in an attempt to silence, intimidate, or punish them into dropping protests/complaints against the plaintiff.

## The Survivor

Meeting with my friend several weeks later, I told him, unfortunately, his experiences with the Rehab were all too common. In fact, what happened to him can and does happen to people in Rehabs in many countries. Thus understanding the need, I decided to write an International Alcohol Drug Resource Guide. The good news is I could use his written narrative to enhance the content being discussed in various chapters of the Resource Guide.

I further explained to him that his name or the Rehab's name could not be mentioned in the book due to the legal settlement. But the names are not necessary. What was important was the story of his experiences with the Rehab. That needed to be told to help others. Hence, in the book he would be known as "the Survivor" and the book would be:

> An International Resource Guide with Alternative Recovery Programs for people with alcohol and/or drug challenges looking for help. With a Self-Help segment in the Guide, How Not to Die in a Rehab, for people who decide to enter a Rehab.

The Survivor was ecstatic and pledged to give his full cooperation with the writing of the Resource Guide. He did.

# Resources

## Non-fully regulated $35 billion-dollar-a-year industry

Horvath, G. (Producer), & Finberg, A. (Director). (2016). The business of recovery [Documentary]. USA: Distribber.

Lanzone Morgan, LLP. (2018). Problems with drug rehab centers. (2018). Retrieved from http://www.lanzonemorgan.com/drug-rehab-center-abuse-cases/problems-with-drug-rehab-centers/

Maryland Addiction Recovery Center. (2017). The underbelly of addiction treatment: A look at the unethical and illegal practices of "saving lives." (2017). RetreivedRetrieved from https://www.marylandaddictionrecovery.com/underbelly-addiction-treatment-unethical-illegal-practices-saving-lives

Munro, D. (2015). Inside the $35 billion addiction treatment industry. Retrieved from https://www.forbes.com/sites/danmunro/2015/04/27/inside-the-35-billion-addiction-treatment-industry/#798fc55017dc

Saavedra, T. (2018). Death in rehab generates $7 million award. Retrieved from https://www.ocregister.com/2018/02/08/death-in-rehab-generates-7-million-award/

Sforze, T. (2018). Legislators taking aim at scams in the drug rehab industry. RetreivedRetrieved from https://www.ocregister.com/2018/04/24/legislators-taking-aim-at-scams-in-the-drug-rehab-industry/

Staff Report, *The Orange County Register*. (2017). The Southern California rehab industry spans the nation. Retrieved from https://www.ocregister.com/2017/05/21/the-southern-california-rehab-industry-spans-the-nation/

## Not-fully trained Rehab employees

Held, M. (2018). What does it mean to be certified, licensed, or accredited in the drug and alcohol treatment industry? Retrieved from https://thriveglobal.com/stories/what-does-it-mean-to-be-certified-licensed-or-accredited-in-the-drug-and-alcohol-treatment-industry/

Szalaviz, M. (2013). Q&A: What really goes on in drug rehabs. Retrieved from http://healthland.time.com/2013/02/15/qa-what-really-goes-on-in-drug-rehabs/

## Rehab problems other countries

Arce, R. (2017). At least 16 murdered in Mexican border state drug rehab center. Retrieved from http://www.breitbart.com/texas/2017/09/27/least-16-murdered-mexican-border-state-drug-rehab-center/

Brown, R. (2016). Canada's private drug rehab industry is unregulated chaos. Retrieved from https://www.vice.com/en_ca/article/5gqd5a/canadas-private-drug-rehab-industry-is-unregulated-chaos

Greenwood, R. (2018). Australia has a drug problem: Ross Greenwood. Retrieved from https://www.9news.com.au/national/2018/04/06/11/44/australia-illegal-drug-economy-booming-ross-greenwood-analysis

Lacey, M. (2009). 17 killed in Mexican rehab center. Retrieved from https://www.nytimes.com/2009/09/04/world/americas/04mexico.html

Ryan, N. (2014). Rehab group reveals top executive salaries…and twelve earn over €200 K. Retrieved from https://www.thejournal.ie/rehab-group-ceo-salaries-executives-1357173-Mar2014/

## SLAAP Lawsuit

Wikipedia: The Free Encyclopedia. (2018). Strategic lawsuit against public participation. Retrieved from https://en.wikipedia.org/wiki/Strategic_lawsuit_against_public_participation

# CHAPTER TWO

# SURVIVOR'S STORY

In my wildest imagination I never thought I would be helping to write a book that would help people around the world. A book with options to help with addictions and save lives. I now realize this book was pre-ordained by fate, destiny, Karma, God, or "everything happens for a reason," take your pick. This book was set in motion by one of those forces the rainy day I walked into my doctor's office. I was depressed and complaining to him I could not sleep because I was going through an extremely rough patch in my life. The patch consisted of a divorce, a classic mid-life crisis, and a loved one's debilitating illness that eventually resulted in their demise. Under the umbrella of these events, I simply could not sleep.

The doctor prescribed 90 tablets of 10 mg valium with multiple refills and instructed me to take one before bedtime.

Thus, started my seven years of addiction to the drug. Compounding my addiction to the prescribed medication, while under its influence my alcohol consumption drastically increased. I was one of the lucky ones. With my addiction, I never wound up in jail, no DUI, and never hurt anybody physically. Hurting other people emotionally is another story.

I am grateful I did not die from my addiction and from what happened to me in Rehab. Not dying, but living, enabled me to participate in writing this book. If this book saves just one life or helps people get sober and/or prevents them from going through what I experienced in a Rehab, then my effort with the book was worth it.

Even though I had a horrific experience with a Toxic Rehab, I feel Steve writes a book that is even-handed and fair. Of course, I know as well as Steve knows, all Rehabs are not Toxic. However, even those that are not, they can turn Toxic under certain circumstances as explained in the book.

### *My Rehab Story*

The story of what happened to me in Rehab is long with many twists and turns. In other words, it takes a while to tell the story from A to Z. I happened to find an outline for a B (bad) movie script on the web. I was amazed to see the outline is an encapsulation of my Rehab experience when you do the following when reading it:

- ▶ Substitute "Bill" for me (Survivor).
- ▶ Substitute "the Gang" for my Rehab.
- ▶ Substitute "the Enforcer" for a lawyer.

▸ Substitute "beating(s)" for the legal paperwork and/or legal proceedings.

### The "B" Movie Outline

Setting: Present day

Working Title: *Gang Gone Deadly*

Main Characters:

Bill: An even-tempered, trusting, spiritual person who always gives people the benefit of the doubt. He is searching for help out of a self-inflicted situation.

The Gang: Polished, well-trained organization with deep, deep pockets filled as a result of doing business with people like Bill. The Gang sets their own rules, are arrogant and vengeful.

Log Line: The hero is a Charles Bronson-*Death Wish* type without the muscles, fighting back against a gang that did him many injustices, including almost killing him. The movie segues into the hero's favor once he gets the attitude of the quote, *"I'm mad as HELL and I'm not going to take this anymore!"* from the classic movie *Network*.

### *Synopsis*

Bill is in big trouble. He thinks the only way out of his trouble is with the help of a Gang. Unwittingly, he picks and pays the wrong Gang to help him. After the gang did not do what they were paid to do and gives Bill a drug that almost kills him, he confronts them.

The Gang does not like to be confronted and sends their highly paid enforcer to intimidate and suppress Bill. The enforcer tells him to leave the Gang alone and move on or he will experience beatings. Bill does not comply with the enforcer's warning and starts to receive beatings. After the first beatings begin, Bill starts a metamorphosis and ultimately fights back with the help of his own hired enforcer and he wins the day.

The full details of my saga with the Rehab are fully explained in the guide in the appropriate chapters.

### Bad Apples

I would like to add this now. I watched a Chris Rock comedy special on Netflix called *Tambourine* while helping with this book. Halfway through his routine, Rock said some jobs and businesses should not have *bad apples*. Then he said, "For example, pilots and airlines." Raucous laughter filled the air, and he then elaborated the reasons why, which I think are self-evident.

I believe the Rehab Industry also cannot afford to have bad apples. After saying that, I sincerely hope this book helps to eliminate the bad apples in the Rehab Industry or, at the very least, helps you spot a bad apple to prevent you from buying it.

# RESOURCE GUIDE ONE

Only I can change my life.
No one can do it for me.

Carol Burnett

# CHAPTER THREE

# GUIDE ONE OVERVIEW

Many studies and reports state the Alcoholic Anonymous (AA) program works successfully for 5% to a high of 10% long term for its members. Depending what you read or believe, this leads to the conclusion that the AA program does not work for all people. New studies are coming out that alternative recovery programs have the same or close to the statistical numbers of people successful with AA.

When I say alternative recovery programs, I am referring to programs that are not based on the Alcoholic Anonymous program which is famously known for their 12-step approach to sobriety. The alternative recovery programs in the guide are not AA programs, although a few of the programs have modified the

AA's steps to fit into their guidance and philosophy. I did include a chapter on the AA program as an option for recovery.

To sum it up, *The International Alcohol Drug Resource Guide* gives alternative recovery options to people not successful with AA. The *Resource Guide* gives them options in finding an alternative recovery program that works for them.

**The Chapters**

The content in each chapter is not meant to be all inclusive. It is intended to give a non-biased synopsis of alternative recovery programs for alcohol and/or drug addiction. The synopsis of a program will help you determine if you want to find out more about it. Think of each chapter as a segment in a travel guide. A travel guide gives you the highlights of a destination. If the highlights resonate with you, you can explore the destination further to determine if you want to go there.

**Online and Offline**

When I say "Offline," I'm referring to a group meeting that is held in a physical locality. When I say "Online," of course, I'm referring to the internet. The majority of alternative recovery programs have Online group meetings, Online Forums, Online Blogs, FB pages, Online help available 24/7, and informative web sites. Some groups even have telephone and Skype meetings available.

All Online and Offline group meetings can be joined by a person anywhere in the world. In addition, with most programs, a person can start their own group meetings Online and Offline. This is great if a person prefers an Offline group meeting and one is not available locally. A person starts their own group meeting with guidance from the program they want to start.

**Terms used in Guide One**

- ▶ Non-12 Step: A recovery program that is not based on the 12 steps used in Alcoholic Anonymous (AA).
- ▶ Fellowship Program: A program a group of people follow to obtain similar goals and at the same time support each other in reaching these goals. All Fellowship programs state they are not professional and do not give medical treatments or medical therapy.
- ▶ Evidence-based treatment (EBT): Rehab programs that use treatments which have been scientifically proven to help addicts recover from their drug and/or alcohol addiction.
- ▶ Secular: Non-religious or non-spiritual program.
- ▶ Non-secular: Spiritual or religious program.
- ▶ Abstinence-Based: Program does not allow alcohol or drug use.
- ▶ Moderation-based: Program allows alcohol use in moderation.
- ▶ Rehab: A facility that requires you to stay on-site for their recovery treatment plan.
- ▶ Intensive Outpatient Program (IOP): A facility that not does not require you to stay overnight for their recovery treatment plan.

## Disclaimer

I do not endorse any of the programs in Guide One, nor was I paid to include them in the *Resource Guide*. The "Member Insights" segment does give biased opinions from group members about their specific program.

# References

### A.A. works successfully for 5% to 10%

Dodes, L., & Dodes, Z. ((2014). The pseudo-science of Alcoholics Anonymous: There's a better way to treat addiction. Retrieved from (https://www.salon.com/2014/03/23/the_pseudo_science_of_ alcoholics_anonymous_theres_a_better_way_to_treat_addiction

Flanagin, J. (2014). The surprising failures of 12 steps. Retrieved from https://www.theatlantic.com/health/archive/2014/03/the-surprising-failures-of-12-steps/284616/

Glaser, G. (2015). The irrationality of Alcoholics Anonymous. Retrieved from https://www.theatlantic.com/magazine/archive/2015/04/the-irrationality-of-alcoholics-anonymous/386255/

Horvath, G. (Producer), & Finberg, A. (Director). (2016). The business of recovery [Documentary]. USA: Distribber.

Munro, D. (2015). Inside the $35 billion addiction treatment industry. Retrieved from https://www.forbes.com/sites/danmunro/2015/04/27/inside-the-35-billion-addiction-treatment-industry/#798fc55017dc

## Alternative Recovery Programs have the same success numbers as AA.

Chabala, T. (2018). SMART, LifeRing, and Women for Sobriety are as effective as AA, study shows. Retrieved from https://www.thefix.com/smart-lifering-and-women-sobriety-are-effective-aa-study-shows

Lopez, G. (2018). Alcoholics Anonymous works for some people. New study suggests the alternatives do too. Retrieved from https://www.vox.com/science-and-health/2018/3/5/17071690/alcoholics-anonymous-aa-smart-lifering-study

## References

https://www.thefix.com/smart-lifering-and-women-sobriety-are-effective-aa-study-shows

https://www.vox.com/science-and-health/2018/3/5/17071690/alcoholics-anonymous-aa-smart-lifering-study

Do not dwell in the past,
do not dream of the future,
concentrate the mind
on the present moment.

Buddha

# CHAPTER FOUR

# LIFERING SECULAR RECOVERY

LifeRing Secular Recovery (LifeRing) is a secular, abstinent, non-12-step program, self-supporting and non-profit organization. It is a network of international support groups Online and Offline, to help people live free of alcohol and other addictive drugs.

**Program Overview**

The only requirement to join LifeRing's program is a new member's willingness to quit alcohol and substance addiction, no matter the drug(s) of choice. It is not anti-religion, and indeed many program members are religious. Their philosophy is you can become clean and sober regardless of your belief or disbelief in a higher power. "Empower your Sober Self" is their slogan.

Program has three basic principles:

- ▶ Sobriety, which is abstinence from alcohol and other addictive substances.
- ▶ Secularity, which means that members can achieve sobriety using their own will power.
- ▶ Self-Empowerment, which means each member is allowed to design his or her own recovery program.

The program teaches there are two voices within you and they are in a constant conflict. The Sober Voice within you represents your Sober-Self and wants you to get out of addiction. The Addiction Voice within you wants you to keep using. When you continue to use, the Addiction Voice has prevailed. The teachings and meetings are all about empowering your Sober Voice, so it can prevail and you become your "Sober Self."

There is not one standard method to the "Sober Self." Many different methods in the program can be used by themselves or in combination to help you stay sober. Motivational interviewing, solution-focused therapy, role-playing methodology, and cognitive behavioral therapy are just a few. Concepts and ideas from other sources and programs can be used if they help a person be his or her Sober Self. The program believes in anonymity and sponsors[1] are not used because each member works out their own personal recovery.

---

1    An AA sponsor is a person who has been abstinent for a long period and who is prepared to support a newly abstinent member.

## Group Meetings

Online and Offline meetings are led by volunteer leaders. The leaders are recovering from their addictions and have gone through the program themselves. Their main job is to guide the group conversation to make sure it is positive and focuses on current situations.

Most group meetings are started by the leader's question, "How was your week?" This one question sparks the dialogue for members to participate in the group meeting. Members are not required to refer to themselves as alcoholics or drug addicts, etc.

Meetings do not to focus on the past problems addictions have caused. The belief is that dwelling on the past does not help the current situation. The meetings use a more positive approach that is centered around the present and how to be your Sober Self. Crosstalk[2] is encouraged in meetings and it is believed this will make the meetings successful. Friends and family are welcome to meetings as long as they are clean and sober. In between meetings, members are contacted through email, phone, and newsletters to keep them motivated to stay with their program.

## Founder

LifeRing was founded by Martin Nicolaus in 1997. Martin was an addict. He recovered after implementing the methods used in LifeRing. Martin draws from his own personal experiences

---

2   Members talking to one another or discussing what someone has just said.

to motivate and inspire others with his work at LifeRing. He has published several books, including "Empowering your Sober Self" and "Recovery by Choice." Although Martin retired in 2010, he still appears occasionally for public speaking engagements and other events.

## Member Insights

*P. C.*

I went to my first LifeRing meeting in October 2007. I found an approach that respects everyone's individuality, indeed urges you to discover what you need to do to maintain your sobriety. LifeRing meetings have helped me express how my struggle with addiction has affected me. I had heard about it before, but was hesitant to attend any meetings or seek help. I thought that I could do it by myself. While I had success, trying to recover by myself left me without any resources or support to assist me when things got difficult. Talking in a group about our short-timer goals the past week and for the future week allowed me to stay focused and to receive helpful tips and new perspectives offered by the group. LifeRing meetings have made my recovery easier—without me needing to rely on outside help or focus on things that don't help me.

*C. W.*

When I found LifeRing on the internet, I knew instantly that I'd found what I was looking for. LifeRing had no meetings anywhere near me, so not knowing what to expect I joined a

LifeRing email group on the internet. It functioned like a slow motion, 24/7/365 support meeting that I could enter or leave whenever I chose without missing anything. It was a perfect fit for me. I participated actively and knew that the "support" piece of the recovery puzzle was in place.

Support isn't the only thing needed, however, and it still took me a good long time to get sober for good. I had to learn things about myself, about the nature of addiction, and about what I needed to change and what I needed to hold on to. LifeRing meetings helped with this. It's been more than 15 years now since I had a drink. I'm not Mr. Happy now—my life isn't filled with joy every minute—but I've regained my health and my self-respect. People entering recovery need to know that there are choices. I'm so glad I made the right choice—LifeRing.

Where there is no struggle,
there is no strength.

Oprah Winfrey

## CHAPTER FIVE

# SECULAR ORGANIZATION FOR SOBRIETY

Secular Organization for Sobriety (SOS) is a non-profit, secular, abstinence-based, non-12 step, self-supporting, Global network of autonomous groups. The goal of the groups is to help people live alcohol and drug free.

**Program Overview**

The program's main philosophy is that to break the cycle of addiction you must:

- ▶ Acknowledge that you have an addiction.
- ▶ Accept that to be addiction free, abstinence is the only way to recover from addiction.

> ► Reaffirm daily that to be addiction free, abstinence is the only way to recover from addiction.

Recovery tools and strategies empower members to break the cycle of addiction are included in the program. The recovery tools and strategies change negative behavior, emotions, and habits to enable a person to become and stay sober. It is acknowledged that genetics can be a contributing factor to addiction, but members are allowed to decide whether alcoholism and drug addiction are diseases or not.

The program's guidelines for sobriety are:

- To break the cycle of denial and achieve sobriety, we first acknowledge that we are alcoholics or addicts.
- We reaffirm this daily and accept without reservation the fact that as clean and sober individuals, we do not drink or use, no matter what.
- Since drinking or using is not an option for us, we take whatever steps are necessary to continue our Sobriety Priority lifelong.
- A quality of life, "the good life," can be achieved. However, life is also filled with uncertainties. Therefore, we do not drink or use regardless of feelings, circumstances, or conflicts.
- We share in confidence with each other our thoughts and feelings as sober, clean individuals.
- Sobriety is our priority and we are each responsible for our lives and sobriety.

- Addiction thrives in isolation; group interaction can promote recovery.

The General Principles of SOS are:

- All those who sincerely seek sobriety are welcome as members in any SOS Group.
- SOS is not a spin-off of any religious or secular group. There is no hidden agenda, as far as SOS is concerned with achieving and maintaining sobriety (abstinence).
- SOS seeks only to promote sobriety amongst those who suffer from addictions. As a group, SOS has no opinion on outside matters and does not wish to become entangled in outside controversy.
- Although sobriety is an individual responsibility, life does not have to be faced alone. The support of other alcoholics and addicts is a vital adjunct to recovery. SOS members share experiences, insights, information, strength, and encouragement in friendly, honest, anonymous, and supportive group meetings.
- To avoid unnecessary entanglements, each SOS group is self-supporting through contributions from its members and refuses outside support.
- Sobriety is the number one priority in a recovering person's life. As such, he or she must abstain from all drugs or alcohol.
- Honest, clear, and direct communication of feelings, thoughts, and knowledge aids in recovery and in choosing nondestructive, non-delusional, and rational approaches to living sober and rewarding lives.

- ▶ As knowledge of addiction might cause a person harm or embarrassment in the outside world, SOS guards the anonymity of its membership and the contents of its discussions from those not within the group.
- ▶ SOS encourages the scientific study of addiction in all its aspects. SOS does not limit its outlook to one area of knowledge or theory of addiction.

Membership is anonymous, and sponsors are not used in the program. The belief in a higher being and/or spirituality is not required for the program to work.

**Group Meetings**

There are Online and Offline group meetings globally plus FB groups. They are led by volunteer Group Leaders. Group leaders can be recovering addicts or professionals in the field of addiction recovery.

Meetings focus on the recovery tools, strategies and guidelines for sobriety. Members have the freedom to choose the tools and strategies that will work for them and set weekly goals that help to maintain their sobriety.

Each group meeting is autonomous and has its own agenda, although they do operate under suggested guidelines for group meetings. It would behoove you to try several groups until you find one with a format that works for you.

There are SOS group meetings for friends and loved ones of the people suffering from addiction.

## Founder

SOS was founded by James Christopher. As an alcoholic looking for recovery, he started his sober journey with Alcohol Anonymous. Unhappy with AA and its spiritual connotations, he wrote about his frustrations with it and how he intended to start a secular recovery group for addiction recovery.

In 1985, Christopher published an article by the name "Sobriety Without Superstition." This article picked up traction and was read worldwide. He then decided it was time to start the secular group he had written about earlier. The first SOS group meeting was held in 1986 in Northwood, California.

Christopher has been clean and sober since 1978 and is the author of the books two books, *S.O.S. Sobriety* and *Unhooked: Staying Sober and Drug-Free*.

## Member Insights

*Judd H.*

I knew to stay sober I needed help, so I found SOS and joined. With the help of SOS, I have learned a tremendous amount myself with by doing so, have re-claimed control of my life and found sobriety. I am happier now than I have been in many years. And I'm present. I truly live in the moment. Now, sobriety isn't easy. I no longer crave alcohol, but occasionally long for the release of the stress in my life. When that happens, I reach out to other members of SOS, and they help me deal with the stress.

And make me laugh and feel good about myself. If SOS worked for me, maybe it can for you. Give it a try.

*K.L.*

I found Sobriety through SOS. And what do I enjoy most about being sober? Life and all it has to offer when you have a clear head. That includes family and work. My marriage is now great. I have a creative employment I really love. And with SOS meetings I have helped others get sober and even lead some group meetings. As an added dividend of my sobriety, my anxiety attacks are gone! Who would have guessed that? After having them most of my adult life. The bottom line is I wake up every day feeling good, ready to face my day. I can truly say, SOS has helped me achieve my sobriety and the benefits that come with it.

**Website**

www.sossobriety.org/

It is in your moments of decision
that your destiny is shaped.

Tony Robbins

Rock bottom
became the solid foundation
on which I rebuilt my life.

J.K. Rowling

# CHAPTER SIX

# SELF-MANAGEMENT AND RECOVERY TRAINING

Self-Management and Recovery Training (SMART Recovery) is an international, secular, largely self-supporting, non-profit, non-12-step program. It has its own 4-Point Program for recovery. The program supports members in staying within the limits they choose for themselves. Many members elect abstinence from one or more substances, but the choice of limits is up to them. The program is for all addictions, including alcohol, all drugs, eating disorders, gambling, sex, and smoking. SMART Recovery labels itself "a mental health and educational program, focused on changing human behavior."

## Program Overview

The SMART Recovery program is based on training oneself to change personal emotions, actions, and negative behaviors to become and stay sober and not dwell upon the past. A 4-Point Program is used to accomplish this. The four points are:

1. Building Motivation.
2. Coping with Urges.
3. Problem Solving.
4. Lifestyle Balance.

The 4-Point Program has a variety of techniques and one tool to help individuals gain independence from addiction and addictive behaviors. Members are encouraged to learn the techniques and use the tool. The techniques and tool are below.

Techniques:

- ► Stages of Change.
- ► Change Plan Worksheet.
- ► Cost/Benefit Analysis (Decision Making Worksheet).
- ► ABCs of REBT[1] for Urge Coping.
- ► ABCs of REBT for Emotional Upsets.
- ► Awareness and Refusal Method.
- ► Hierarchy of Values.
- ► Brainstorming.
- ► Role-playing and Rehearsing.

---

1   A cognitive-behavioral (thinking/doing) psychotherapy. REBT stands for Rational Emotive Behavior Therapy.

▸ USA (Unconditional Self-Acceptance).

Tool:

▸ DISARM (Destructive Images and Self-talk Awareness and Refusal Method).

The program also has a philosophy that some members' beliefs about addiction can be damaging in their quest for sobriety. A few of those beliefs are:

- I am powerless.
- After the first drink you have to lose all control.
- I've tried and failed, so I can't do it.
- I need alcohol to cope.
- Because I've tried to quit and failed, I'm no good.

The program helps members eliminate these damaging beliefs.

## Group Meetings

SMART group meetings are available Online and Offline internationally, including the United States, Australia, Canada, Ireland, the UK, and Denmark. On-Line forums are available and open 24/7. This allows members to interact anytime they need help.

Most meetings are open to the public unless they are specifically designated "private." The group meetings are led by two types of leaders. One leader has over 30 hours of intense SMART Recovery program training and is called a "Facilitator." The other leader is called a "host" who undergoes a less rigorous training.

There are different dynamics of group meetings, depending on what type of leader is in charge. The hosted meeting tends to have more structure than a facilitated meeting. You should try different group meetings with both types of leaders to see which meeting you are most comfortable with.

Group meetings focus on self-empowerment so the members can become free of their addiction(s). Hence, the 4-Point Program is discussed at each meeting along with various tools and techniques that fit in with a member's need.

No one is labeled an "alcoholic," an "addict," "diseased," or called "powerless" in group meetings. Open discussion between group members and the Facilitator/Host is encouraged. Sponsors do not exist in the program because of the self-empowerment philosophy of the program that states "individuals have the power within themselves to find the path to recovery."

## Founders

In 1985, a for-profit program named Rational Recovery was founded by Lois and Jack Trimpey. The Rational Recovery meetings began to grow and spread throughout the early 1990s. In 1993, a non-profit program, Rational Recovery Self-Help, Inc., was established by Dr. Joe Gerstein. In 1994, Rational Recovery Self-Help, Inc. ended its relationship with Rational Recovery. The name was changed to SMART Recovery. Joe Gerstein and Rob Sarmiento created the acronym "Self-Management and Recovery Training." 1996 was when the 4-Point Program was established in SMART Recovery.

## Member Insights

*Autumn G.E.*

As an agnostic, I struggled to use Narcotics Anonymous to break my crack and meth addiction, doing everything recommended daily with very little success. After a few years of stationary wheel-spinning, I found SMART Recovery on a desperate late-night Internet search. Volunteers in the 24/7 chat room and message boards answered my questions and shared what had helped them. The Toolchest on the site gave me practical tools I could download for free. I used the ones that made sense to me, and I went to local meetings to meet and talk to folks in person. That was four years ago. Since then, I've made many of the usual human mistakes—to learn new things and improve skills—and I've had a total of four slips on meth. Celebrating two years sober for the first time recently felt amazing! Today, I volunteer online and facilitate a weekly face-to-face meeting that makes me feel important to a good group of people who matter to me. Life is still tough, but really rewarding at the same time. I have learned to push at the edges of my unhealthy habits and work toward healthier choices each day.

*Kim B.*

I have been an addict for 24 years. My drug of choice was always pills. I never cared which type either. My mother passed away in January of 2016. At that time, I turned to meth daily for two-and-a-half years. In April, I attended my first SMART Recovery Group. I was so amazed by the welcome and non-judgement of everyone. For the first time in my life, I had a glimpse of hope that I could get clean. With the four simple principles of SMART Recovery, I learned how to no longer be a slave to my thoughts, feelings, or urges. I learned I have the power (not powerless) to stop and do a cost-benefit analysis on my next action.

I have been impressed with SMART from the beginning because of no one judging me and where I am at in my recovery. Everyone I have interacted with always had my best interest in mind. Knowing I'm not powerless has been the turning point in my recovery. Believing I have control over my thoughts and actions are key for me...believing I can be successful without a sponsor telling me everything I'm doing wrong. All of these things have been a major key in my success. I have never been clean for this long in the past 24 years. Finally, I believe in myself again. I wouldn't be where I'm at today without SMART Recovery showing me I am enough! SMART Recovery gave me my life back!

Life is very interesting...in the end, some of our greatest pains become our greatest strengths.

Drew Barrymore

Remember that just
because you hit bottom doesn't
mean you have to stay there.

Robert Downey Jr.

# CHAPTER SEVEN

# REFUGE RECOVERY

Refuge Recovery is an international non-profit, abstinence-based, non-12-step, secular program based upon Buddhist philosophy and teachings. The program's goal is to help those struggling with addiction find a personal healing path to sobriety. The program works with all addictions.

**Program Overview**

The Refuge Recovery program is based on facets of Buddhist philosophy and teachings. It is a spiritual program, but a God or Higher power reference is not used. The program teaches all living and breathing beings are capable of healing and overcoming suffering with their own innate power. This innate power is facilitated in the program by Four Truths of Refuge Recovery, which are based on the Four Noble Truths.

The Eight-Fold Path is very in-depth and the program states it will lead you to higher awareness, freedom from pain, freedom from suffering and thus freedom from addiction(s).
The Four Noble Truths are:
1. Suffering
2. The cause of suffering
3. The end of suffering
4. The path

The Four Truths of Refuge Recovery:
1. Addictions create ongoing suffering.
2. Addiction is caused by craving and repetitive behavior.
3. Recovery is possible if you are ready.
4. The Eightfold Path is the path to recovery.

Part of the program is to study and practice the eight steps in the Eight-Fold Path as stated in The Four Truths of Refuge Recovery. The Eight-Fold Path is very in-depth and the program proclaims it will lead you to higher awareness, freedom from pain, freedom from suffering and thus freedom from addiction(s). The eight steps are:
1. Understanding and Perfect Vision: To understand and have perfect vision means to be aware of a given situation as it is. It involves accepting that suffering and dire situations are inevitable throughout a life and they must

be confronted with compassion rather than substance use and temporary pleasure.

2. Intention: To have intention is to have goals and motives. In recovery, one must be committed to their path of recovery to avoid suffering.

3. Communication and Community: To communicate is to practice being as honest as possible by admitting struggles and sufferings that may be imminent. Clear, concise, honest, humble, compassionate speech is the goal.

4. Right Action: Creating an ethically-sound foundation for life. This means abstaining from behaviors that may negatively impact or harm oneself or others.

5. Proper Livelihood and Service: To practice ethical soundness. The focus is on generosity, kindness, and service to the others to create positive change. Resources should be acquired in a non-harming manner and should be used wisely.

6. Effort: Think commitment and discipline. Recovering from an addiction requires putting as much effort and energy as possible into the path. This requires mindfulness, meditation, and awareness.

7. Mindfulness Meditation: To fully experience life, one must consistently be present in the moment. It allows one to become aware of their emotions, abilities, and mental faculties.

8. Concentration Meditation: Involves focuses on a single object such as a mantra or breathing pattern. Positive meditations relate to compassion, kindness, forgiveness,

and love which will assist a person to reach the right state of mind.

In the program "The Four Truths of Refuge Recovery" and "Eight-Fold Path" work hand-in-hand.

## Group Meetings

Group meetings are available Online, Offline, and via phone meetings worldwide. FB group pages are available and FB live. Workshops and videos Online are also available for members to study in between meetings. It appears the latest internet technology is available for Online communications with members. Group meetings function independently under the umbrella of Refuge Recovery guidelines. The group meeting guidelines are:

- The group's health and well-being are of utmost importance. Personal recovery depends on connection with a healthy, safe, confidential, and stable community.
- Each group's core intention is to welcome and support those who are seeking recovery.
- Groups are to be peer-led. For groups to be healthy and successful, there must be a rotating leadership and democratic decision-making process.
- Group leaders do not act in the capacity of recognized Buddhist teachers, but are trusted volunteers who serve the group for a designated period of time.

▸ Refuge Recovery is an abstinence-based program. Trusted volunteers are expected to maintain abstinence from all recreational drugs, alcohol, and process addictions.

▸ Each group operates independently, except in matters affecting other groups or Refuge Recovery as a whole. Just as individuals endeavor to live in accordance with the Eightfold Path, so should each group adhere to these Guiding Principles to maintain group integrity.

▸ There are no fees for Refuge Recovery membership. Each group is responsible for its own finances, relying on the generosity of its members.

▸ Ethical conduct can and should be practiced on a group level. As a group, we refrain from violence, dishonesty, sexual misconduct, and intoxication.

▸ Our core principles are mindfulness, compassion, forgiveness and generosity. We commit to being open and accessible to all who seek refuge.

New members can be of any religion and family members are welcomed to the group meetings.

## The Founder

Noah Levine was instrumental in starting Refugee Recovery. At a young age he was incarcerated with three felony convictions. It was then he realized he needed help. He was aware of Buddhism teachings from his father and started working with them to become sober. Noah has remained sober since that time. He has become a teacher of Buddhism and author of *Refuge Recovery: A Buddhist Path to Recovering from Addiction*, and he works with incarcerated youth and adults. He has retreats and classes about the power of Buddhist meditation and philosophy.

## Member Insights

*Jet P.*

When I first started to drink and use drugs, it made it easy to connect with other people. In the end of my addiction I was using drugs and alcohol to connect with myself and everything else was gone. Meditation and the process of Refuge Recovery taught me how to reconnect with myself so I can connect with others. Refuge is a comprehensive recovery approach that has given me both education about my drug abuse and, more importantly, practical tools to deal with it.

*F.T.L.*

Refuge Recovery shows me the path to the end of the suffering created by addiction and gives me the tools I need to navigate that path on a daily basis. The tools of the program and the teachings of the Buddha allow me to experience ordinary life in a relieving and refreshing way—a way which is totally different from any experience I've had in recovery—or in life—up to this point. In the Refuge program, ancient wisdom and modern knowledge reinforce one another and form techniques to build a solid foundation for living. If you have suffered as a sensitive human being in this world as I have, then I believe you will find great relief in mindfulness, meditation, and the application of the teachings to your recovery and to your life.

If we are facing in the right direction,
all we have to do is keep on walking.

Zen proverb

# CHAPTER EIGHT

# WOMEN FOR SOBRIETY

Women for Sobriety (WFS) is an international, secular, non-profit addiction recovery program for women with substance use disorders. The program is based on 13 Acceptance Statements. Only women are allowed in WFS meetings because the program's focus is on women's gender specific needs with substance abuse issues and recovery.

## Program Overview

Women for Sobriety believes when women have addictions, they lose their self-esteem and all confidence in their lives. The majority of times, they believe, the root cause of a woman's addiction is lack of self-value and self-worth. To change all this and help women overcome their addictions, WFS offers the New Life Program.

The New Life Program helps women identify the specific problems that cause their addiction and methods to heal so they can become sober and live sober. The core of the New Life Program works with the four key elements for behavioral changes and 13 Acceptance (or Affirmations) Statements. When both are implemented by a woman, they will provide her a path to a new way of life and sobriety.

The four key elements for change:
1. Positive reinforcement (approval and encouragement)
2. Cognitive strategies (positive thinking)
3. Letting the body help (relaxation techniques, meditation, diet and physical exercise)
4. Dynamic group involvement

The 13 Acceptance Statements[1]:
1. I have a life threatening problem that once had me.
2. Negative thoughts destroy only myself.
3. Happiness is a habit I am developing.
4. Problems bother me only to the degree I permit.
5. I am what I think.
6. Life can be ordinary or it can be great.
7. Love can change the course of my world.

---

1    Reprinted with permission from Women for Sobriety, Inc., PO Box 618, Quakertown, PA 18951; 215-536-8026; womenforsobriety.org © WFS Inc.

8. The fundamental object of life is emotional and spiritual growth.
9. The past is gone forever.
10. All love given returns.
11. Enthusiasm is my daily exercise.
12. I am a competent woman, and I have much to give life.
13. I am responsible for myself and for my actions.

WFS has a motto that encapsulates the program, "We are capable and competent, caring and compassionate, always willing to help another, bonded together in overcoming our addictions."

## Group Meetings

WFS is for women who are engaged in recovery from substance use disorders. Participation is free. The only requirements to attend are to be a woman over 18 and seeking sobriety from alcohol and/or other drug addictions. Group meetings are anonymous. All group meetings are led by a certified moderator (CM). CMs must be sober at least one year, have extensive knowledge of the WFS New Life Program, and be certified by the WFS organization.

Group members avoid labeling themselves as addicts or alcoholics and, instead, refer to themselves as competent women. Being competent women, WFS believes program sponsors are not needed. Group meetings focus on women improving their self-esteem and reducing guilt, but never admitting they are powerless. In the meetings, members discuss topic provided by the

CM. Each member is encouraged to include at least one positive behavior or event from the previous week. Cross-talk is allowed, but members are discouraged from sharing drug or alcohol addiction stories, called drunkalogues[2].

Women for Sobriety has Online and Offline group meetings worldwide; plus, they have Online chatrooms that are available where women can interact 24/7.

**Founder**

Women for Sobriety was started by Jean Kirkpatrick, Ph.D. in 1975. Dr. Kirkpatrick had used the AA program successfully for 3 years, but when she attempted to return after a 13-year absence, she was unable to reconnect with the 12 Steps. With the help of meditation, research into the science of alcoholism, and reading of metaphysical offerings such as Emerson, Thoreau, and New Thought literature, she eventually regained sobriety on her own.

Now sober, she organized 13 affirmations that she had found especially helpful into the Acceptance Statements and developed the New Life Program which is used in WFS. As a sociologist, Dr. Kirkpatrick believed that women had different needs in recovery from men, and she developed WFS to speak directly to women's gender-specific needs.

---

2   When group members recount stories of the damage alcohol and drugs did to them.

## Member Insights

*Melissa B.*

When I found Women for Sobriety, I read a set of statements that made me feel empowered. I felt lost and low, and I had little belief and faith in my abilities. I posted to the WFS forum and was met with empathy, non-judgement, and kindness. Compassionate responses flowed from ladies that I could not see, yet I could feel their warmth, their genuine caring for me. I found a group of ladies that understand my struggles, that are there for me through the highs and the lows, women that are proud of me and celebrate my success. Slowly my pride and self-belief have crept back, now I actually LIKE who I am. I know I can do this. I have begun the process of trusting who I am again. One day, I look forward to being able to provide a Women for Sobriety group in my area. I now understand why we call each other Sisters!

*Tiffany M.*

When I first found Women for Sobriety, it was after yet another relapse in yet another month in yet another year of trying to get sober. I halfheartedly started reading though the website to see what would make this program "different." I started reading through the 13 Statements, and pretty soon it felt like a light bulb went on in my head. In order to change my life, I needed to change the way I think. For some reason, the idea that I had everything I needed to be able to recover from the disease of alcoholism and that it was residing right in my own mind, made

complete and total sense. I immediately began reading the Statements daily and choosing one to work on. Along with going on
the WFS forum and connecting with other women in recovery,
attending face-to-face meetings here in my area, and participating in the online chats, I have found the key to my success. I am
so grateful to Jean Kirpatrick, who as a woman seeking sobriety
but unable to find something that worked for her, decided to
go against the grain and create her own way. And now there are
thousands of women who are getting sober and living a happy
life because of her New Life program, WFS. Myself included.

To forgive is to set a prisoner free and discover that the prisoner was you.

Lewis B. Smedes

If you can quit for a day,
you can quit for a lifetime.

Benjamin Alire Sáenz

# CHAPTER NINE

# EMOTIONS ANONYMOUS

Emotions Anonymous (EA) is a global, non-profit, secular program with a modified 12-step program for emotional illness and addiction recovery. EA's program intent is to empower members to manage their mental health and/or addiction challenges and lead productive lives.

## Program Overview

Emotions Anonymous is a program for relief and recovery of emotional issues. The program is not only for people struggling with addictions, it's for any person with emotional issues that needs help. Having said that, many of the emotional issues the program helps with can be the result of and/or the cause of alcohol and drug addiction.

Below are nine emotional issues the program provides support. The list is not all inclusive.

1. Depression
2. Excessive anger
3. Anxiety
4. Excessive resentment
5. Panic
6. Phobias
7. Grief
8. Low self esteem
9. Compulsive behaviors

EA is nonprofessional program, but it can be used in conjunction with professional mental health therapy and professional addiction recovery. It is not necessary to be seeking or having professional help to attend EA group meetings. The program is spiritual, with an emphasis on a Higher Power. The program works equally well for members with or without any religious beliefs.

> The program has 12 steps the members follow, and they are identical to the AA 12 steps[1] except Step 1 has been modified to: "We admitted we were powerless over our emotions, that our lives had become unmanageable." And in step 12 the words "to alcoholics" is omitted.

---

1    See Chapter on AA the 12 Steps.

The program and meetings are basically built on the 12 concepts of EA which are:

1. We come to EA to learn how to live a new way of life through the 12 step program of Emotions Anonymous which consists of Twelve Steps, Twelve Traditions, concepts, the Serenity Prayer, slogans, Just for Todays, EA literature, weekly meetings, telephone and personal contacts, and living the program one day at a time. We do not come for another person—we come to help ourselves and to share our experiences, strength, and hope with others.

2. We are experts only on our own stories, how we try to live the program, how the program works for us, and what EA has done for us. No one speaks for Emotions Anonymous as a whole.

3. We respect anonymity. No questions are asked. We aim for an atmosphere of love and acceptance. We do not care who you are or what you have done. You are welcome.

4. We do not judge; we do not criticize; we do not argue. We do not give advice regarding personal or family affairs.

5. EA is not a sounding board for continually reviewing our miseries, but a way to learn to detach ourselves from them. Part of our serenity comes from being able to live at peace with unsolved problems.

6. We never discuss religion, politics, national or international issues, or other belief systems or policies. EA has no opinion on outside issues.

7. Emotions Anonymous is a spiritual program, not a religious program. We do not advocate any particular belief system.

8. The steps suggest a belief in a Power greater than ourselves. This can be human love, a force for good, the group, nature, the universe, God, or any entity a member chooses as a personal Higher Power.

9. We utilize the program; we do not analyze it. Understanding comes with experience. Each day we apply some part of the program to our personal lives.

10. We have not found it helpful to place labels on any degree of illness or health. We may have different symptoms, but the underlying emotions are the same or similar. We discover we are not unique in our difficulties and illnesses.

11. Each person is entitled to his or her own opinions and may express them at a meeting within the guidelines of EA. We are all equal. No one is more important than another.

12. Part of the beauty and wonder of the EA program is that at meetings we can say anything and know it stays there. Anything we hear at a meeting, on the telephone, or from another member is confidential and is not to be repeated to anyone—EA members, mates, families, relatives or friends.

The program also has 12 Traditions which are identical to AA's 12 Traditions[2], but EA has been substituted for AA in the Traditions.

---

2   See Chapter on AA the 12 Traditions.

## Group Meetings

There are global Online, face to face meetings and 24/7 Online Forums, Skype and phone meetings. All you need to join EA is the desire to work on your issues. EA group meetings are free and open to the public unless they are designated as "special" or "invitation only." Group meetings are organized and led by volunteers. Some volunteers have suffered from emotional issues and/or addictions, while others have not. The volunteers can be professional medical providers, but no one is considered to be a 'leader' in a group-all share in the responsibility of managing the meetings and staying true to the EA materials. Sponsors do exist in the EA program.

Group meetings provide self-empowerment and emotional support to the members. In addition, the meetings discuss the teachings and learning materials of the program. There are general group meetings and specialized meetings. The specialized meetings are about specific topics.

The philosophy of all group meetings is "Through weekly support meetings, we discover we are not alone in our struggles. Although we each might have different symptoms, the underlying emotions are the same or similar." EA group meetings are known for their open and frank discussions, non-judgmental environment of love and acceptance with no arguing or criticism, and that all are welcome.

## Founder

Emotions Anonymous was officially started July 22, 1971, by Marion Flesch. Marion had suffered anxiety attacks for decades. A friend suggested that she attend an Al-Anon[3] meeting, hoping the anonymous sharing of her experiences would help her. This meeting was her inspiration to start her own group. Marion started with simple groups that expanded and the groups evolved to become Emotional Anonymous.

Marion worked as a teacher, bookkeeper, secretary, clerk, office manager and at one time, an accountant. Later in life, she became a certified chemical-dependency counselor through the University of Minnesota and then started working on a Master's degree. Unfortunately, she had to stop at age 80 due to health concerns.

## Member Insights

*P.I.*

I tried to stop drinking. I assumed my drinking was because I was shy and lonely. After a weeklong binge, I found E.A. on line. I read all the site's pages. It all made sense to me. My emotions were out of control. I was drinking because of my shyness and perceived loneliness. And to compound matters, my drinking was out of control. I was heading towards suicide. Unfortunately,

---

3    A resource and support group for adult relatives and close friends of alcoholics. Al-Anon is available to interested individuals, even if the alcoholic does not participate in the group.

there was no E.A. meeting where I lived, so I was active with E.A. online.

Seven years later I am sober and deal with my emotions daily—thanks to E.A.

*Mary R.*

It is my belief that without E.A. I would not be clean today and not have a handle on my anger issues and panic attacks. The support from E.A. groups online and offline when I needed it, have been a blessing to me. Joining E.A. two years ago has made a profound, positive difference in my life. I understand E.A. might not work or be a fit for every person seeking help, but I do recommend at least give E.A. try—especially if you have addiction challenges compounded by emotional issues.

If things go wrong, don't go with them.

— Roger Babson

# CHAPTER TEN

---

# MILLATI ISLAMI

Millati Islami (The Path of Peace) is an international, non-secular, non-profit, abstinence based, Islamic 12-step, self-help program. It's for people who want to be free of any and all addictions.

**Program Overview**

Program promotes itself as a fellowship of men and women united on "The Path of Peace" with a common goal to recover from addictions of mind and body altering substances. They accomplish this with a 12-step program based upon Islamic principles. The program has an in-depth manual that outlines the Millati Islami 12-step recovery process. The manual is supported by the Qur'an and Hadith (sayings and practices) of

Prophet Muhammad. The manual includes worksheets and is a free to download with the 12 steps on the Millati Islami World services web site.

The program states, "Members look to Allah for guidance on The Path of Peace (Millati Islami). And as recovering addicts we strive to become rightly guided Muslims, submitting our will to the will and service of Allah. We begin the submitting process through the practice of Al-Islam (peaceful submission to the will of Allah) in our daily lives."

Millati Islami Twelve Steps to Recovery are:

1. We admitted that we were neglectful of our higher selves and that our lives have become unmanageable.
2. We came to believe that Allah could and would restore us to sanity.
3. We made a decision to submit our will to the will of Allah.
4. We made a searching and fearless moral inventory of ourselves.
5. We admitted to Allah and to ourselves the exact nature of our wrongs.
6. Asking Allah for right guidance, we became willing and open for change, ready to have Allah remove our defects of character.
7. We humbly asked Allah to remove our shortcomings.
8. We made a list of persons we have harmed and became willing to make amends to them all.
9. We made direct amends to such people wherever possible, except when to do so would injure them or others.

10. We continued to take personal inventory and when we were wrong promptly admitted it.

11. We sought through Salaat[1] and Iqraa[2] to improve our understanding of Taqwa[3] and Ihsan[4].

12. Having increased our level of Iman (faith) and Taqwa, as a result of applying these steps, we carried this message to humanity and began practicing these principles in all our affairs.

The Millati Islami also has 12 Islamic Traditions that go with the 12 steps. They are:

1. Shahadah: We bear witness that there is no God but Allah, and Muhammed is the last messenger of Allah.

2. Personal recovery depends upon Millati Islami unity. Believers are friends and protectors of one another.

3. For our individual and Jamaat (group) purpose there is but one ultimate authority which is Allah (God, the source from which all originates).

4. Requirements for participation are a desire to stop using and willingness to learn a better way of life.

5. Each Jamaat (group) should be autonomous except in their adherence in to these traditions.

6. Our primary Jamaat (group) purpose is carrying out Al-Islam as the message of recovery to those who still suffer (Dawah).

---

1   Prayer service in Islam.
2   Reading and studying.
3   God consciousness; proper Love and respect for Allah.
4   Though we cannot see Allah, He does see us.

7.  Problems of money, property, and prestige must never divert us from our primary purpose.

8.  Every Millati Islami Jamaat (group) should be self-supporting but may accept sadaqa (voluntary charity) without attached obligations or promises to donating parties.

9.  We may create service boards and committees directly responsible to those we serve.

10. The Millati Islami name aught never be drawn into public controversy.

11. Our public relations policy is based upon attraction before promotion. The criterion for both are decided by Jamaat (group), Taqwa, and Ihsan.

12. Iman (faith) is the spiritual foundation of all our traditions, reminding us to place principles before personalities.

## Group Meetings

There are Offline meetings, FB pages for daily interaction with members and conference call meetings worldwide. Meetings are led by a group member. All people are welcomed to meetings. There are Speaker meetings and Round-Robin meetings which can be open discussion or topic meetings. Most group meetings include discussing the Islamic 12 steps and the 12-step manual. The underlying focus of meetings for the members is, as recovering addicts, how they can strive to become rightly guided Muslims in the service of Allah.

**Founders**

Millati Islami was started in Baltimore, Maryland, in September, 1989, by Zaid Imani. Zaid wanted to incorporate the Islamic way of life with the traditional twelve-step approach to the treatment of addiction.

In the fall of 1992, Zaid met Bilal Ali. Bilal Ali was a facilitator of Jama'at Al Tauba, a Washington, D.C., recovery group for Muslims. After the meeting, Bilal Ali announced that the Jama'at Al Tauba group had decided to become a part of the Millati Islami program. In January of 1993, the Millati Islami recovery program went international.

## References

http://www.millatiislami.org/

http://web.archive.org/web/20060701100703/http://www2.islamicity.com:80/al-muminun/MIFAX/mifax.htm

Attitude is a little thing
that makes a big difference.

Winston Churchill

# CHAPTER ELEVEN

# ADDICTION RECOVERY PROGRAM

The Addiction Recovery Program (ARP) is non-profit, international, and non-secular. It uses its own 12-step program to help people addicted to drugs and alcohol to become addiction free and live a productive life.

## Program Overview

The Addiction Recovery Program is based on overcoming addictions through Jesus Christ and His Atonement[1]. It is a modified

---

1 Theology. The doctrine concerning the reconciliation of God and humankind, especially as accomplished through the life, suffering, and death of Christ.

12-step program that incorporates gospel principles for recovery and healing. The belief is that with the Savior's help you can overcome addictions, find new meaning to life, and be fully healed.

The 12 steps of the Addiction Recovery Program are based on gospel principles. The steps contain explanations of principles, practical suggestions for applying those principles, and "understanding" questions relating to each step.

The Addiction Recovery 12 steps are:
1. Honesty
2. Hope
3. Trust in God
4. Truth
5. Confession
6. Change of Heart
7. Humility
8. Seeking Forgiveness
9. Restitution and Reconciliation
10. Daily Accountability
11. Personal Revelation
12. Service

There is a free in-depth, downloadable Addiction Recovery Program Guide that leads a person through the program. Each step has a Key Principle and includes instructions for studying and understanding the step and how to put the step into action. The Addiction Recovery Program Guide is available in over 30 languages and English Braille. Additional free support material for the program is on the web site. This includes videos, library, mP3 files, weekly pod casts, and daily inspirational quotes.

Also available on the web site is a downloadable 104 page support guide: Help for Spouses and Family of Those in Recovery.

## Group Meetings

Group meetings are available worldwide Offline and there are group meetings that are conducted by phone. Fb pages and website support are available for the program 24/7. Meetings are open to all in need of help with recovery. In meetings, it is not required you label yourself an addict or an alcoholic.

Meetings focus on ARP's 12 steps of recovery and are led by a group leader, called a facilitator. Facilitators are fully trained in the Addiction Recovery Program before can they can lead a meeting. On the web site are videos of group meetings so you can get an idea if the meetings are for you.

## Founder

The Addiction Recovery program is operated under LDS Family Services which changed its name from LDS Social Services in 1995. LDS Family Services is a nonprofit corporation owned and operated by The Church of Jesus Christ of Latter-day Saints. The international web site with all support material was put online in May 2012.

## Member Insights

*S.F.P.*

I believe the Addiction Recovery Program is an incredibly useful tool for any type of addiction. It has made a difference in my life and introduced me to people who have been an inspiration and help to me on my path to find happiness. With this program I celebrate eleven years of recovery plus ten years of a happy marriage. I attend at least three meetings weekly: one that I facilitate and the others to help me continue in my recovery process. Through the process of rebuilding my life, with the program I have learned humility. I've been able to make reconciliations, legally and personally. I have had to ask many for forgiveness and pay my debt to society, but I am now able to let go of the past. I believe the program will help any person that will adhere to it.

*M.J.*

I have been in the program a year and a half. In the program I started to deal with the pain of the divorce, and I finally began working through my addictions and other issues I had buried since my early teenage years. I attend Addiction Recovery Meetings, even though I had been sober for the year and a half. The meetings, however, helped me learn more about the program. Through counseling, the Addiction Recovery Program, and continued activity in the church, I learned to rely on my faith in order to get through the most difficult time of my life. I have learned that the Atonement is not only for repentance; it can heal our broken hearts and teach us to forgive others who have hurt us. I will stay sober with the program's help.

**Website**

https://addictionrecovery.lds.org/?lang=eng

First step is to have to say you can.

Will Smith

# CHAPTER TWELVE

# ALCOHOL HELP CENTER

The Alcohol Help Center is a non-secular interactive web site with free self-help programs and guidance online for people who either want to stop or cut down their drinking. The program can be modified for use of drugs.

**Program Overview**

The program has many resources, such as Cognitive Behavioral Therapy (CBT) exercises, guidance pages, and work books to help members create and succeed in their own recovery plans. Below are the resources available on site.

*Interactive Programs:*
- ▶ Blood alcohol Calculator
- ▶ Members Goals
- ▶ Email Program
- ▶ Daily Dairy
- ▶ Getting Started
- ▶ Do I drink too much
- ▶ Check Your Drinking
- ▶ The first two weeks
- ▶ Cutting back
- ▶ Cost and Benefits
- ▶ Triggers
- ▶ High Risk Situations
- ▶ Changing the Rules
- ▶ Rewarding Yourself
- ▶ Member's Goals

*Dealing with Difficulties Information:*
- Dealing with Desires
- Saying No Thanks
- New Relationships
- Medications
- Tracking Temptations
- Emergency Plan

*Maintenance Guidance:*
- ▶ Support Team
- ▶ Keeping Active

- ▶ Healthy Eating
- ▶ Coping with Stress

Interactive Programs can be done in any order and at your own pace. This enables you to create your own personal recovery plan.

**Group Meetings**

Access to the program online is 24/7. Online anonymous support groups are available and moderated by an expert staff member. There are enhancements to the support groups which include the ability to add avatars, emoticons, or generate a personal profile. There is an option to communicate with a moderator one-on-one if needed. Motivational emails and instant messaging between program participants are available.

**Founder**

The Alcohol Help Center was first launched in 2005. It was created by Evolution Health Inc. under the guidance of Dr. Trevor van Mierlo. Evolution Health builds digital health programs that change a patient's behavior. Dr. Trevor van Mierlo is a digital economist and leading authority in the science of online engagement.

## Member Insights

*Janet D.*

Hello! Today marks two years that I decided not to let alcohol control my life and my only regret is that I didn't do it long ago. I gave up something that had become a focal point of my life and I don't miss it. As a past everyday drinker I no longer wait for that "OK" time to drink. On outings with friends, I no longer wonder if I will be able to drink the way I want. I'm no longer careful with what I eat during the day to save my calories for the large amount of alcohol that would be consumed later that day. There are so many more benefits, but these are the ones that really stick out in my mind when thoughts of having a drink pop into my mind. I was a frequent visitor to this site and it helped me get to where I am today. Everyone that comes here has their own story so each needs their own plan. Good luck to everyone here in achieving their goal. It is possible no matter how hard it feels at times.

*Avery M.*

Thank you to everyone on this brilliant site. It has inspired me so much, and today is my 25th day without alcohol!! I cannot begin to tell you how much better I feel both physically and mentally. I can see the change in the mirror, and family and friends have commented on how much better I look. I am due to be married in June and my partner has also given up drinking (although he didn't have a problem with it!) to support me. I work from home as a freelance portrait artist, which was part of the problem as it was easy to open a bottle! I used to think it actually helped my work if I had a few drinks. The truth is after one or two, my attention would stray to just sitting and drinking the rest of the bottle! In the past three weeks I have completed commissions which have been waiting for a while and started new paintings which would never have got done as I wouldn't have been sober enough. I realize I have a long way to go, but filling in my diary every day with those zeros is a real sense of achievement for me, so thank you everyone for all of your help and support. xxx

**Website**

http://www.alcoholhelpcenter.net/

Struggle you're in today
is developing the strength
you need for tomorrow.
Don't give up.

Robert Tew

# CHAPTER THIRTEEN

# HARM REDUCTION, ABSTINENCE, MODERATION SUPPORT

Harm Reduction, Abstinence, Moderation Support (HAMS) is a secular, non-spiritual, non-profit, non-12-step program for people who want to reduce alcohol-related risks, reduce amounts consumed, adopt moderation, or abstain in their consumption of alcohol. The philosophy of the program is "It does not matter how much or how little you drink; if you want to make a change you are welcome here."

**Program Overview**

The program is designed to reduce the risks and harm caused by drinking an excess of alcohol. It allows you to set your own goal for safe drinking, reduced drinking, or quitting alcohol altogether. HAMS recognize that many people change by gradual increments rather than all at once and therefore encourages any steps toward positive change, no matter how small." The program stresses that every person is independent, unique in his or her recovery. Hence, members can set their own drinking moderation goals and plans with the 17 elements.

The Seventeen Elements are the foundation of the HAMS program. They do not have to be followed in any specific order to work, nor do all the elements have to be completed. You can choose to work with some of the elements or all of them. What works for you to support your recovery plan is what is important. The 17 elements devised for the HAMS recovery program are as follows:

1. Do a cost-benefit analysis (CBA) of your drinking. Individuals weigh the pros and cons of their alcohol consumption.

2. Choose a drinking goal: safer drinking, reduced drinking, or quitting altogether. Individuals choose which direction they want to pursue.

3. Learn about risk ranking and rank your risks. List your most harmful behaviors and rank them according to their risk factor which helps focus on significant problems first.

4. Learn about the HAMS tools and strategies for changing your drinking habits.

5. Make a plan to achieve your drinking goal. A plan plays a significant role in achieving a drinking goal. Sample plans are available on the website.

6. Use the alcohol-free time to reset your drinking habits.

7. Learn to cope without booze. For some, alcohol is the only option when dealing with stressful situations and this element makes such individuals realize that there are other ways to deal with such scenarios.

8. Address outside issues that affect drinking. Most of the time, external and outside pressures cause alcohol addiction, and thus they should be recognized and resolved.

9. Learn to have fun without booze. Want to have fun? It can be done without alcohol.

10. Learn to believe in yourself. The most important thing is to have self-confidence and to truly believe that you are capable of quitting something that harms you.

11. Use a chart to plan your drinks and track your drinking behaviors each day.

12. Evaluate your progress, honestly report struggles, and revise plans or goals as needed. Modifying your plans over time is essential.

13. Practice damage control as required.

14. Get back on the horse!

15. Graduating from HAMS, sticking around, or coming back.

16. Praise yourself for every success. Do not belittle your own achievements at any cost.
17. Move at your own pace.

Sample recovery plans on the web site will give you an idea how to develop your own. If you are concerned that you might have withdrawal symptoms by drinking less, a page on the main website has information about how to taper off alcohol.

**Group Meetings**

In addition to Online and Offline support groups, online services offer chatroom meetings, Facebook groups, podcasts, email groups, and a forum where experts can give advice and interact with members. Group leaders are called Facilitators. They are volunteers from the group. The Facilitator is there to guide the meeting to make sure the rules and platform of the group meeting are followed by all. During the group meetings, members share their experiences and how they are progressing. They can also give their opinions of the ongoing topic. The underlying principle of meetings is not to be judgmental of another.

**Founder**

Kenneth Anderson is the CEO and founder of the HAMS Harm Reduction Network. Kenneth has a masters in psychology and substance abuse counseling from the New School for Social Research. He is the author of *How to Change Your Drinking:*

*A Harm Reduction Guide to Alcohol.* In his book, he explains why harm reduction is the most suitable way of overcoming alcohol addiction and the principles to accomplish that. HAMS is based on these principles.

## Member Insights

*C.V.*

I have benefited from the HAMS site and info from the Yahoo HAMS group. The info on the website is easy to understand and extremely helpful—there is something to learn and to help us on every page. (I have re-read many of the pages.) The group on the Yahoo email list are awesome supporters of one another and a great source of shared information as well. Nothing but good has happened to me since I found HAMS and have been able to cut my heavy drinking level way down, learn how planning and tracking really help, and I have enjoyed several days of abstinence as well. Thank you for all you have done for me.

*Trevor R.*

Being in HAMS has reinforced to me that I deserve dignity. It has taught me that every human being has dignity and should be treated as such, whether they are addicted or not. Harm reduction means giving voice and hope to those who might otherwise not have a second chance. HAMS does not ignore or condemn me for my drinking. It meets me where I am at "right now," therefore it is practical and can be used in my everyday life. HAMS recognizes all the factors that go with any addiction/alcoholism. The

HAMS program is my solution to harmful and dangerous drinking of alcohol. By following tips in the HAMS program, I have been successful in reducing the rate and amount of consumption by a significant degree. My quality of life has improved, my time better spent, and personal relationships improved. It really works for me. I am happy with the results.

**Website**

http://www.hams.cc/

Sometimes the people around you
won't understand your journey.
They don't need to, it's not for them.

Joubert Botha

Nothing is impossible, the word
itself says I'm Possible.

Audrey Hepburn

# CHAPTER FOURTEEN

# MODERATION MANAGEMENT™

Moderation Management (MM) is a behavioral change program to reduce alcohol drinking. The program also helps identify problems in drinking habits and patterns that may lead to addiction. It is a secular, non-profit, non-12-step program. It is the premise of the program that "Moderation is a reasonable, practical, and attainable recovery goal for many problem drinkers."

**Program Overview**

The program does not require a person to stop drinking[1]. It's up to you to make the make the choice of moderation or abstinence.

---

1    MM does have a group if person wants to abstain on their site called mmabsers.

The program states abstinence can only come through reduction and moderation, and eliminating the habit should not be the first aim.

The program's focus is on changing individual drinking habits so drinking is not harmful. This is accomplished with the Nine Steps Toward Moderation. It is not necessary to follow the steps in any order. You just need to make sure you are progressing towards the goal of moderation and/or abstinence.

Nine Steps Toward Moderation are:
1. Attend meetings or on-line groups and learn about the program of Moderation Management.
2. Abstain from alcoholic beverages for 30 days and complete steps three through six during this time.
3. Examine how drinking has affected your life.
4. Write down your life priorities.
5. Take a look at how much, how often, and under what circumstances you have been drinking.
6. Learn the MM guidelines and limits for moderate drinking.
7. Set moderate drinking limits and start weekly "small steps" toward balance and moderation in other areas of your life.
8. Review your progress and update your goals.
9. Continue to make positive lifestyle changes and attend meetings whenever you need ongoing support or would like to help newcomers.

The program has Values and Assumptions that helps a person understand and use the program.

The Values are:

- ► Members take personal responsibility for their own recovery from a drinking problem.
- ► People helping people is the strength of the organization.
- ► People who help others to recover also help themselves.
- ► Self-esteem and self-management are essential to recovery.
- ► Members treat each other with respect and dignity.

The Assumptions are:

- • Problem drinkers should be offered a choice of behavioral change goals.
- • Harmful drinking habits should be addressed at a very early stage, before problems become severe.
- • Problem drinkers can make informed choices about moderation or abstinence goals based upon educational information and the experiences shared at self-help groups.
- • Harm reduction is a worthwhile goal, especially when the total elimination of harm or risk is not a realistic option.
- • People should not be forced to change in ways they do not choose willingly.
- • Moderation is a natural part of the process from harmful drinking, whether moderation or abstinence becomes the final goal. Most individuals who are able to maintain total abstinence first attempted to reduce their drinking, unsuccessfully.

- Moderation programs shorten the process of "discovering" if moderation is a workable solution by providing concrete guidelines about the limits of moderate alcohol consumption.

There is a downloadable comprehensive pdf on their website called "Guide to Moderation Management Steps of Change" to help with the program. Also available on the site, is an online drink planner that helps track alcohol consumption.

## Group Meetings

Online and Offline group meetings, Online forum, chat rooms open 24/7, phone meetings, and MM's own unique Listserv, which is an email forum, are available. Some groups are open to the public and other groups are for members only.

Group leaders are non-professionals who use the MM program. The group leader does have to meet the following MM guidelines: minimum age of 21, no charges related to alcohol in the past six months or any pending court-orders, knowledge of the MM recovery program and its material, and completed a 30-day abstinence period at least once.

Group meetings can discuss various topics. Most will focus on some elements of the MM program. Discussion of group members' goals and achievements with the programs take place. Cross-talk is allowed as members discuss and share their stories.

## Founder

Moderation Management was founded by Audrey Kishline in 1994. It was created as an alternative non-abstinence recovery program for non-dependent problem drinkers, that is drinkers with their first goal to cut back on the amount of alcohol they are drinking and a second goal to prevent problems in their lives from excessive alcohol consumption.

Moderation Management today is led by a group of people who themselves were once victims of excessive alcohol consumption problems. Before his retirement, this included The Habit Doc, Dr. Marc F Kern, who was part of the board of directors of Moderation Management and the founder of The Moderation Management Movement.

## Member Insights

*L.D.M.*

I joined MM in Oct 2008. Daily drinker of 1–2 bottles of wine. I read everything on the MM site, got RD, and started planning. In 3 weeks, I was abusing 3–4 days/week—something I never thought I could achieve. Baby steps really helped.

Initially my main goal was to be able to take or leave a drink. I despaired that that day would never come. Thanks to MM, I have met that goal and more! I abs 3–5 days a week and am BTB on days I do drink. I do on occasion go over, but this is the exception, and I am OK with this. I can go out to eat, a party, or whatever and it is no longer in my thoughts to get hammered!

Before, that was a given. I no longer wake up in the early AM hours thirsty and miserable.

It did take work, but it is doable and sustainable. So, yes, moderation is possible for some of us.

*R.S.*

When I found MM, I didn't believe I had a disease. I didn't concede that I had an addictive personality and frankly I didn't want to give up fine wine. I knew I was drinking too much and it would eventually kill me. I didn't believe I was powerless over alcohol, and I didn't want to abstain forever. It took me two years of practice, patience, and persistence, and I finally have the MM tools ingrained into my lifestyle. I can have a perfectly enjoyable meal with water or tea. Now my social drinking is quite moderate. I park my drink, drink water in between, and eat a large meal before drinking. I never drive under the influence. I owe all of these life skills to MM. Moderation Management guides participants, but those participating are there because they want to be there, not because they have to be there. Like me.

**Website**

http://www.moderation.org/

# References

http://www.moderation.org/about_mm/whatismm.html

Recovery give me a spiritual anchor.

Eric Clapton

It is during our darkest moments that
we must focus to see the light.

Aristotle

# CHAPTER FIFTEEN

# SEVEN WEEKS TO SOBRIETY

The Seven Weeks to Sobriety program is based on taking natural chemicals (vitamins/minerals) to recover from alcoholism. The addiction recovery is facilitated by taking vitamins/minerals that restore chemical balance to the brain and body caused by addiction. This is called "biochemical repair." The program is detailed in the book of the same name, *Seven Weeks to Sobriety*, by Joan Mathews Larson, Ph.D.

**Program Overview**

The program states psychological problems do not lead to addiction. It is abuse of alcohol that disrupts brain chemistry and causes psychological problems to manifest. Talk does not fix this. Biochemical repair must occur, and that's what the program does.

The program shows you:

▶ How to determine if you are alcoholic and what chemistry-type you are.

▶ How to break your addiction with minimal discomfort.

▶ How to determine and replace key natural chemicals (vitamins/minerals) to eliminate alcohol-induced symptoms such as anxiety, depression, insomnia, cravings, and unstable mood swings.

The program promises:

• Physical repair, including the brain and central nervous system.

• Restoration of the immune system and memory.

• Stabilization of glucose metabolism.

• To rebuild adequate adrenal stamina.

• To become addiction free.

Some people combine the program with another recovery program of their choice, which does have group meetings (talk) as part of recovery. This maximizes their odds for complete sobriety.

**Online Support**

Groups, forums and FB pages are available Online for support of the program. People discuss the pros and cons of the program in detail in these venues. Many web sites on line have the vitamins and minerals recommended to be taken in the program for bio-chemical repair.

**Founder**

The *Seven Weeks to Sobriety* book was published in 1997 by Dr. Joan Mathews-Larson. The best-selling book describes the program of the same name. Book supports Dr. Mathews-Larson's beliefs that addiction and mental health problems arise from lack of nutrients/chemicals. The doctor holds a doctorate in nutrition and is the founder and executive director of the highly esteemed Health Recovery Center in Minneapolis.

**Member Insights**

*Jimmy C.*
I'd finally give up and drink again to ease the withdrawal night-mare. I tried the program with the recommended supplement support. I took the supplements as detailed for a full day, and by the end of the day, I prepared for sleep expecting the worse. I woke 10 hours later without waking once! Perhaps the best sleep I ever had since being a baby. I went through this second day like a Super Hero that I and my coworkers noticed. I couldn't believe it. Day 2, 3, 4, 5...the same and even better. Cravings, insomnia, panic, anxiety, palpitations, irritability, jerks...not once in weeks. I have absolutely no desire to drink, don't feel like I'm missing anything, and am better able to fully immerse and enjoy myself

with my friends. I didn't think the program would work for me, but it did. Maybe you too. Best of luck.

*R.T.*

This program will save your life!! It did mine! In the summer of 2015, I was overwhelmed with stress at work, and bought some beer. I knew where this would lead, non-stop drinking every night. I then started the vitamin/mineral program. Right away, it reduced the craving for alcohol. What a difference now I am sober. I plan on doing the maintenance vitamin/mineral program explained in program. I will be taking these vitamins/minerals for the rest of my life. I recommended the program to anyone struggling with alcohol as well.

**Website**

https://sevenweekstosobriety.wordpress.com/
http://www.joanmathewslarson.com/

If I continued it, I was really going to sabotage my whole life…I don't drink or do drugs anymore. Being sober helps a great deal.

Bradley Cooper

The best preparation for tomorrow
is doing your best today.

H. Jackson Brown, Jr.

# CHAPTER SIXTEEN

# NIACIN DETOX PROGRAM

Niacin Detox is a program that cleanses the body of drug toxins (including alcohol) stored in the fat cells of the body. It accomplishes this with a niacin protocol. The program claims a person can recover from an addiction if their body is detoxed and cleansed. It is usually used simultaneously with a fellowship recovery program for a better chance of success of recovery, although there are success stories of the program freeing people of addictions when used by itself.

**Program Overview**

Niacin is vitamin B3 and is created naturally in your body. In the program you take a higher dose of niacin than that recommended by the FDA[1]. You combine this with moderate to heavy exercise.

---

1   USA's Federal Food and Drug Administration.

This starts lipolysis (break down of fats with the toxins) so you excrete the toxins naturally, mainly through sweating. The doses of niacin are different in the various programs available. All the programs recommend checking with your doctor before you start as higher doses of niacin and exercise could create health issues.

The basic protocol of the program is:

- Establish what dose of niacin is safe for you.
- Exercise soon after dosing with the niacin. This increases the body's heart rate which helps spread the niacin throughout the body, which breaks down the toxins stored in the fatty tissue.
- During and after exercise, the broken-down toxins are forced out of the body by sweating. A shower should be taken soon after exercise to wash away the toxins secreted. A shower makes sure the toxins are not reabsorbed back into the body.
- Recommend taking a sauna after exercising to produce more sweating.
- Drink plenty of water before, during and after exercise to replace the water you will be sweating out.
- Add healthy oils to your diet. This helps replace the toxic fat cells removed.
- Eat large amounts of fruits and vegetables while on the program so your colon has plenty of fiber to help eliminate the toxins released by the program.

As a side note, when taking niacin, most people within five to ten minutes experience a temporary sensation of heat or a flushing effect throughout the body.

## Online Support

Online groups and forums offer support and discuss the pros and cons of a niacin detox program. Niacin detox programs can be found Online. You can pick one to use that seems right for you. Most niacin programs have a variation of the protocol I have outlined. The main difference of each program is the niacin dosage. I have put link to one of the most popular programs at the end of the chapter.

## History

There is no direct founder of the niacin detox program, but The New Life Detoxification, part of the International Narconon Rehab program, has given it the most notoriety, good and bad. The Narconon Rehab program is based on scientology. Scientology was founded by L. Ron Hubbard. The following is a quote from their web site. This gives a voice to the premise of niacin detox programs.

"The New Life Detoxification is another unique aspect of the Narconon program. It is based on the discovery by L. Ron Hubbard that drug residues apparently remain trapped in the body's fatty tissues and may be reactivated even years after the individual has ceased taking drugs. The harmful mental and physical effects of taking drugs do not end even when the person stops taking drugs. Therefore, a vital step is to get drugs out of the body and end their mental and physical effects on an individual's life."

**Niacin Detox Program Caveats**

As mentioned before, the program has helped people overcome addiction, but you should be aware of the following caveats before starting the program.

- Doctors who subscribe to niacin therapy generally advise beginning at the recommended daily dose of 30 milligrams and then building up slowly.
- The National Institutes of Health (NIH) in the USA reports that high doses of niacin can cause adverse effects.
- NIH concludes that niacin at doses in excess of 3,000 milligrams can result in liver problems, gout, digestive tract ulceration, heart dysrhythmias, blindness, high blood sugar, and even stroke.
- Niacin should never be taken in doses exceeding 500 mg per day. This about the maximum level of "flushing" that the body can take.
- Overdose of niacin can be extremely dangerous and even fatal. Starting off with a smaller amount of niacin and working up if the desired effects do not occur is strongly recommended.
- People who experience pain from flushing may take aspirin about 30 minutes before beginning their niacin intake.

## Member Insights

*M.O.*

My experiences with the Niacin Detox have been most profound. I am a member of Life Ring, but I was missing something in keeping my sobriety. I did the Detox, and it was Amazing! That was the key to what I was missing. With the Detox, I was able to use a sauna. I feel this made the Detox more effective. If you can, I recommend using a sauna like I did. I whole heartily recommend incorporating the Detox with whatever program you are using. It will give you the edge you need on your sober journey. As for the Niacin Flush, you will adjust to it.

*J.R.T.*

The Niacin Detox program was just great. Although, this is my second try with it. The first one I did not stick with because the flush was a little intense for me. I adjusted the dosage the second time around and all is ok. I believe the Detox has helped me stay off drugs for the last six months. You should give it a try. You have nothing to lose with it, but everything to gain. I do attend group meetings, and it seems most of the members that try the Detox have success with the program like me. The only thing I would say, start out slow with the Niacin and find the right dosage that works for you.

## Website

http://www.flexyourbrain.com/niacin-detox-program/

Put your heart, mind, and soul
into even your smallest acts.
This is the secret of success.

Swami Sivananda

# CHAPTER SEVENTEEN

# THE SINCLAIR METHOD

The Sinclair Method (TSM) is a prescription drug protocol program. Its purpose is to reduce the consumption of alcohol and eventually achieve abstinence. The program can be used by itself or in conjunction with any recovery program. It is claimed TSM is equally effective with or without a recovery program. The drug used in TSM is also used in other protocols to address drug addiction.

**Program Overview**

The TSM works by gradually removing and then eliminating the reward of drinking. Once the reward of drinking is removed, the person loses their interest in drinking alcohol. This is done by a process called "Pharmacological Extinction." Pharmacological Extinction happens by taking a prescription drug naltrexone or nalmefene. Both drugs have the effect of an opiate blocker on the brain.

The TSM protocol for Pharmacological Extinction is this. Take naltrexone or nalmefene two hours before your first drink of the day. Then proceed to drink as you normally would. naltrexone (or nalmefene) chemically disrupts the body's behavior/reward cycle causing you to drink less instead of more. Over a period of several months, it is claimed you will reduce your urge to consume large amounts of alcohol. Extinction usually occurs within nine months. Although with some people it will take over twelve months. Detoxification will happen naturally during the extinction process.

Five TSM steps recommended with the program are:
1. Understand and think about addiction in an entirely new way.
2. Check the severity of the problem and find out if you need help.
3. Work with a doctor to obtain a prescription for naltrexone or nalmefene.
4. Learn about alcoholic beverage measures and keep a record of your drinking and craving as you begin your journey through de-addiction. As you take naltrexone or nalmefene before drinking alcohol, you become de-addicted—your craving and drinking levels decline gradually.

5.  Up to nine months—in some cases after twelve months—
    you will be cured. Your goal is to stay cured once you
    have completed the program.

Taking naltrexone or nalmefene without drinking will result in
a small decrease in craving but will not result in extinction. You
must drink alcohol with the drug to achieve extinction. There are
international web sites that give you guidance where to obtain
prescriptions for naltrexone or nalmefene.

**Online Support**

The program offers Online support groups, web sites, forums,
and FB pages where people interact with each other about using
TSM. The interactions include discussions before starting the
program, during and after the program, and the results of the
program. Suggestions for how and where to get the prescription
for TSM are included in the discussions.

**Founder**

Dr. John David Sinclair started his research in America during
the 1960s. He established the "alcohol deprivation effect" as a
driving force in alcohol addiction. He later moved to Helsinki,
Finland, to take his research forward using specially bred rats
genetically predisposed to becoming alcoholic. He developed
The Sinclair Method during the 1980s.

**Member Insights**

*Julie G.*

I am grateful for TSM, and I have no words to describe how happy I am now. I started to control my drinking, and I quit drinking during the week, moving to weekend sessions only. I also started to drink as late as possible, which can be seen in the last weekend of my drink diary where units are very low. My long-term goal is to become abstinent, but I am focusing first to decrease my drinking. I couldn't be much happier than now. I don't feel like having a drink. I can do my stuff and don't think about drinking. TSM was a Godsend.

*A.P.*

For me The Sinclair Method has proved a remarkably effective way to deal with a problematic relationship with alcohol. One of the great benefits of The Sinclair Method is that you take the pill and sort yourself out. There is no need for meetings, and confessional outpourings, and picking over the detritus of your problem with alcohol. You just take the pill, drink, repeat, and get better. My advice? If you're using TSM for your physical issues, but need some more human support, try a meeting online that will work for you.

**Websites**

https://www.the-sinclair-method.com
https://cthreefoundation.org/find-a-physician

Sobriety was the greatest
gift I ever gave myself.

Rob Lowe

Change your thoughts
and you change your world.

Norman Vincent Peale

# CHAPTER EIGHTEEN

# IBOGAINE TREATMENT PROGRAM

The Ibogaine Treatment Program reduces and eliminates withdrawal symptoms and cravings experienced by opioid addicts trying to get clean. It can also be used in treating dependence on other addictive substances including alcohol. If withdrawal symptoms and cravings are eliminated, recovery can be successful. After going through the Ibogaine Treatment Program, it is recommended joining a fellowship group or seeking individual therapy to maintain recovery.

## Program Overview

During and after a program treatment, withdrawal symptoms subside and drug cravings diminish. Also, during the treatment, the person usually discovers why he or she has a need to use drugs or alcohol. This discovery or enlightenment has been called "a reset switch for life."

The program's protocol usually follows the four steps below. With some programs, there is a little variance with the steps.

1. The person goes into to a quiet room with low lights and relaxing music.
2. A catheter is inserted for fluids and a heart monitor hooked up to keep track of vital signs during the treatment.
3. Once steps one and two are done, the person takes a dose of ibogaine. After sixty minutes or so, the ibogaine psychoactive effects kick in.
4. A support person is always present with the person during the ibogaine treatment, to help and monitor vital signs.

## Three Stages of Treatment

There are three classic stages when ibogaine is ingested, and they are:

1. The first 4 to 8 hours of the treatment are called the Acute Dream stage. Withdrawal symptoms and cravings go away during this time. This stage is dreamlike because of

the psychoactive effects of ibogaine. Most people during this stage report they receive insights about their addictions—why they use, the harm drugs are causing them and their family, what they need to do to stop using, etc. Some people state during this time they get an overview of their whole life, from childhood to present day. An overview of what went wrong and what went right. Vomiting can happen during this time. It is brought on by movement. It is advised to move only when necessary during this stage.

2. After the Acute Dream Stage, a person enters into an Evaluative Stage that can last for up to 20 hours. During this stage, people reflect on their personal understanding of the insights that manifested during the Acute Dream Stage. With these understandings and the disappearance of withdrawal symptoms and cravings, a recovery plan can be formulated and implemented with focused motivation.

3. Following the Evaluative Stage, the person enters a Stimulation Stage that can last up to 72 hours. The body and mind are fatigued but still stimulated during this time from the first two stages. Sleep is difficult. Sedatives or sleeping pills can be administered during this stage because sleep is needed to rejuvenate the person.

Some individuals may require a follow-up treatment for reinforcement over the next 12 to 18 months.

## Online Support

Online groups, forums, and blogs discuss the pros and cons of the Ibogaine Treatment Program. The pros and cons include the experiences and feedback from people who had the treatment.

The possession and sale of ibogaine is illegal in the US, Belgium, Switzerland, Denmark and Sweden. In the rest of the world, ibogaine is either legal or non-regulated. In countries where it is banned, citizens are forced to travel to countries where it is legal to gain access to a treatment program. Ibogaine treatment clinics are available legally in Mexico, Canada, the Caribbean, Central and South America, South Africa, Norway, the Netherlands, the UK, and other countries in Europe.

## History

In the 19th century, explorers first witnessed iboga (ibogaine) being used in African spiritual ceremonies. The first botanical description of the Taberna, the iboga plant was published in 1889.

In the early 1990's, the US National Institute on Drug Abuse (NIDA) began the development of ibogaine in pre-clinical animal trials. Next, trials on human subjects were conducted by Dr. Deborah Mash at the University of Miami. The results confirmed that ibogaine decreases the self-administration of stimulants, opiates, and alcohol, as well as causes a significant reduction in the withdrawal symptoms from opiates.

## Ibogaine Caveats

Ibogaine can decrease coordinated muscle movements and cause tremors during a treatment. Toxicity complications with an ibogaine treatment can happen, although most of the time they are due to previous health issues (primary heart) and other drug interactions with ibogaine. A person with heart issues should be careful in deciding to take ibogaine.

## Ibogaine Insights

*Joel L.*

Before I tried Ibogaine, I had completely given up hope of ever getting clean. I had tried 12-step programs and rehabs, and I was never able to stay clean more than a week on my own. After 10 years of drug abuse, I began to accept that I would live the last days of my very short life addicted to opiates. When I heard about Ibogaine, I decided that very second that I was going to try it. I went home, researched, and next thing I knew I was on a plane to Mexico. Immediately after treatment, I could tell something had changed. My mind wasn't racing, thinking about my next fix anymore. Actually, I wasn't thinking about drugs at all. The cravings and addict mentality seemed almost like a faint memory or a bad dream. For the next few months I was able to live a craving-free life, and I took this time to work on myself trying to build a wall between me and my addiction. If I had not found Ibogaine, I highly doubt that I would be here today.

*Dmitry V.*

I had tried everything between going to traditional rehabs, detoxes, but nothing helped. As soon as I got out I was right back to where I had left off. Ibogaine was absolutely life changing! I never thought I would be able overcome my prescription drug addiction because I could not tolerate the withdrawal sickness. Ibogaine for me was a life-changing experience. It helped me realize some very important things such as why I use drugs, and it showed me the way that my actions affected the people who love and care about me. I can truly say from the bottom of my heart I feel like a brand-new person after Ibogaine. Ibogaine is the most helpful thing that I have ever come across, and I absolutely encourage anybody who is struggling with addiction to give it a try because it will change your life.

# References

Wikipedia: The Free Encyclopedia. (2018). Ibogaine. Retrieved from https://en.wikipedia.org/wiki/Ibogaine

Staff Report, The Third Wave. (2018). *The Essential Guide to Ibogaine.* Retrieved from https://thethirdwave.co/psychedelics/ibogaine/

Levinson, J. (2018). Americans going abroad for illegal heroin treatment. Retrieved from https://www.bbc.co.uk/news/world-us-canada-43420999

Lee, J. (2018). Ibogaine for opiate addiction treatment: Miracle cure or illegal and dangerous? Retrieved from https://www.choosehelp.com/topics/addiction-treatment/ibogaine-for-opiate-addiction-mircale-cure-or-illegal-and-dangerous

The initial journey towards sobriety is a delicate balance between insights into one's desires for escape and abstinence from one's addiction.

Debra L. Kaplan

The undertaking of a new
action brings new strength.

Richard L. Evans

# CHAPTER NINETEEN

# ALCOHOLICS ANONYMOUS

Alcoholics Anonymous (AA) is a global, abstinence-based, 12-step program. It's non-profit, spiritual, and secular, but has strong references to a Higher Power and God in its program. It is a program to help individuals overcome their addiction to alcohol. The program is the basis for recovery treatment for many Rehabs around the world. Alcoholics Anonymous is grandfather of all recovery programs.

**Program Overview**

The program is based upon the *Alcoholics Anonymous* book. The foundation of the program is the 12 Steps which the members work through. The program is also well known for its members telling their trials and tribulations of alcoholism during group meetings.

The program states there is not a cure for alcoholism, and members can never return to normal drinking. The only way to stay sober is to abstain from alcohol by keeping physically, mentally, and spiritually healthy. This health is achieved by going to AA group meetings and using the program.

The program does advocate members having a sponsor. A sponsor in the program is considered a coach or mentor who will assist a member with working through the 12 steps. The sponsor also gives support and guidance on the program when the member needs it.

A key element and focus in the program is spiritual growth, which helps members become clean and sober. Agnostic, atheist, Christian, etc., it makes no difference for the program to work, but you have to decide upon your own Higher Power for spiritual growth.

### The 12 Steps[1]

The 12 steps of the program were designed to be worked on one at a time in sequence. Each Step builds on the other, and they are worked through in a person's own time frame. A person can

---

1  The Twelve Steps and Twelve Traditions are reprinted with permission of Alcoholics Anonymous World Services, Inc. ("A.A.W.S.") Permission to reprint this material does not mean that A.A.W.S. has reviewed and/ or endorses this publication. AA is a program of recovery from alcoholism only—use of AA material in any non-AA context does not imply otherwise.

spend as much time as needed on a step before moving to the next. The Steps are:

1.  We admitted we were powerless over alcohol, that our lives had become unmanageable.
2.  Came to believe that a Power greater than ourselves could restore us to sanity.
3.  Made a decision to turn our will and our lives over to the care of God as we understood Him.
4.  Made a searching and fearless moral inventory of ourselves.
5.  Admitted to God, to ourselves, and to another human being the exact nature of our wrongs.
6.  Were entirely ready to have God remove all these defects of character.
7.  Humbly asked Him to remove our shortcomings.
8.  Made a list of all persons we had harmed and became willing to make amends to them all.
9.  Made direct amends to such people wherever possible, except when to do so would injure them or others.
10. Continued to take personal inventory and when we were wrong promptly admitted it.
11. Sought through prayer and meditation to improve our conscious contact with God *as we understood Him*, praying only for knowledge of His will for us and the power to carry that out.
12. Having had a spiritual awakening as the result of these steps, we tried to carry this message to alcoholics, and to practice these principles in all our affairs.

## The 12 Traditions

The program also has 12 Traditions which are guidelines how AA groups and members should interact with each other and the public. The 12 traditions have been modified and used by many other Recovery Fellowship programs in the world. The short form of the 12 Traditions are:

1. Our common welfare should come first; personal recovery depends upon AA unity.

2. For our group purpose there is but one ultimate authority—a loving God as He may express Himself in our group conscience. Our leaders are but trusted servants; they do not govern.

3. The only requirement for AA membership is a desire to stop drinking.

4. Each group should be autonomous except in matters affecting other groups or AA as a whole.

5. Each group has but one primary purpose—to carry its message to the alcoholic who still suffers.

6. An AA group ought never endorse, finance, or lend the AA name to any related facility or outside enterprise, lest problems of money, property, and prestige divert us from our primary purpose.

7. Every AA group ought to be fully self-supporting, declining outside contributions.

8. Alcoholics Anonymous should remain forever non-professional, but our service centers may employ special workers.

9. AA, as such, ought never be organized; but we may create service boards or committees directly responsible to those they serve.
10. Alcoholics Anonymous has no opinion on outside issues; hence the AA name ought never be drawn into public controversy.
11. Our public relations policy is based on attraction rather than promotion; we need always maintain personal anonymity at the level of press, radio, and films.
12. Anonymity is the spiritual foundation of all our traditions, ever reminding us to place principles before personalities.

## Group Meetings

Group meetings are available Online and Offline globally along with 24/7 Online forums. Meetings are either closed or opened. Closed meetings are for AA members only, or for those who have a drinking problem and "have a desire to stop drinking." Open meetings are available to anyone interested in Alcoholics Anonymous. Non-alcoholics may attend open meetings as observers.

Meetings are led by a leader elected by the group. Group meetings have different topics. Here are just a few examples: Speaker meetings, Speaker/Discussion meetings, Big Book Meetings, Step Meetings, Topic Discussion and Open meetings. The most common meetings that AA is known for are the Open meetings. That's where members tell their personal stories of their addictions and where they are at now.

## The Founders

In 1939, *Alcoholics Anonymous*, called the "Big Book" was written and published by two men who were the co-founders of the program. William Griffith Wilson (Bill W.) was a stockbroker. Robert Holbrook Smith (Dr. Bob) was an American physician and surgeon. The AA program is based on the teachings of this book.

Bill W. was the first of the two to get sober and he was a member of the Oxford group, a sober fellowship that focused on spiritual growth for healing and recovery. It is believed his experience with the group helped Bill W. write *Alcoholics Anonymous*. Dr. Bob found inspiration with the success of Bill W. sobriety and achieved it himself with Bill W's. help. They teamed up to work with alcoholics and the program AA was born.

## Member Insights

*John S.*

I became desperate to do something about my drinking. I got the shakes and sweats if I couldn't get my drink, but I hated it. I was so miserable I just wanted to end it all. I didn't care how, I just wanted it to stop. That's when I joined AA and asked for help. With AA's help I chose the sobriety route and started to attend meetings regularly. I have to be honest and say that the first year was hard, but, year on year, my life has changed for the better. I've been sober for just over six years now and can honestly say that I've got back most of what drink took away from me. However, over the six years of my sobriety, I've gained things in my life that no amount of money could buy. I have a little two-year-old grandson who loves to play with toy cars with his granddad, especially in the toy garage that Granddad had great fun making. He also thinks that Granddad is the best person to head for if he needs comforting after a fall or wants a comfy pair of arms to fall asleep in. This is what no money can buy. Thank you, AA.

*Sally B.*

People that are not "alcoholic" just don't understand. In AA I don't feel like I'm different any more. I have something to belong to. I have found new meaningful friendships. I am also reminded if I ever start to think I can drink like "normal" people, I will end up right back where I came from. Best of all, I found that by following a few simple suggestions on a daily basis, the desire to drink alcohol has completely disappeared. I have discovered that I can solve, or at least cope with, any problem that comes along today by using the tools I found in the fellowship of Alcoholics Anonymous. The people in AA really care about what happens to me and I have a life way beyond my dreams. I have been able to get my life back on track and make up for a lot of things I felt guilty about in the past. My one small regret is that I enjoy my life so much today that I wish I had done something about my drinking problem a little bit earlier.

**Website**

https://www.aa.org/

# RESOURCE GUIDE TWO

## CHAPTER TWENTY

# GUIDE TWO OVERVIEW

Guide Two gives you comprehensive guidance on "How Not to Die" in a Rehab. This guidance includes:

- ▶ Exposing the problems in the Rehab Industry.
- ▶ Why some Rehabs are Toxic.
- ▶ How Toxic Rehabs can harm you physically, mentally, emotionally, and financially.
- ▶ How to avoid Toxic Rehabs.
- ▶ Survivor's cautionary narrative of his true story of how he almost died in a Toxic Rehab.
- ▶ Comprehensive guidance on how to select a Non-Toxic Rehab if you need to enter one.

**International Big Business**

Private Rehabs in the USA have been estimated to be a $35 billion-dollar-a-year (and growing) industry. When you start adding the currency from Rehabs from other countries to that number, like Canada, United Kingdom, Australia, etc., you have an astronomically lucrative international industry.

The story I tell in this guide, with the assistance of Survivor, is about the USA Rehab industry. Other countries around the world are having some, if not all, the same challenges in their own Rehab industry, including weak or nonexistence laws and regulations. In fact, many Rehabs in other countries mirror USA Rehabs because they are so profitable.

When you read about Toxic Rehabs, be aware this is an international problem, and what happened to Survivor could happen in any Rehab. Chapter 31, "Selecting a Non-Toxic Rehab," can be used anywhere.

# References

### $35 billion-dollar-a-year industry

Muro, D. (2015). Inside the $35 billion addiction treatment industry. Retrieved from https://www.forbes.com/sites/danmunro/2015/04/27/inside-the-35-billion-addiction-treatment-industry/#798fc55017dc

### Minimum laws regulations

Held, M. (2018). What does it mean to be certified, licensed, or accredited in the drug and alcohol treatment industry? Retrieved from https://thriveglobal.com/stories/what-does-it-mean-to-be-certified-licensed-or-accredited-in-the-drug-and-alcohol-treatment-industry/

Henry, J. (2018). State shuts down Pasadena-based 'Celebrity Rehab' center over death, repeated violations. Retrieved from https://www.ocregister.com/2018/08/04/state-shuts-down-pasadena-based-celebrity-rehab-center-over-death-repeated-violations/

Horvath, G. (Producer), & Finberg, A. (Director). (2016). The business of recovery [Documentary]. USA: Distribber.

Sforza, T. (2018). Addiction industry executives face off with lawmakers on Capitol Hill. Retrieved from https://www.ocregister.com/2018/07/24/addiction-industry-executives-face-off-with-lawmakers-on-capitol-hill/

# CHAPTER TWENTY-ONE

# TOXIC REHABS

There are over 14,000 Rehabs in the USA that affect the lives of millions of people. What is unusual about an industry this large? No Federal agencies hold the industry accountable. No performance standards are in place to force Rehabs to prove their recovery programs actually work. To add to this, there are no mandatory Federal-standard certification programs for recovery addiction counselors.

The bottom line is Rehabs can make their own rules. And some Rehabs prefer to conduct business in the shadows without public scrutiny. Rehabs in the shadows protect themselves from legal problems with high-priced lawyers who can skillfully manipulate privacy laws. The Rehab Industry has been notoriously labeled by whistle blowers as "The Wild, Wild West."

In the following chapters I expose the issues that create problems in the unregulated Rehab industry. I label these problems Toxic. Below are some of the most common issues that occur in Rehabs with Toxic problems.

- ▸ Fraud
- ▸ Negligence
- ▸ Wrongful death
- ▸ Wrongful medication
- ▸ A failure to provide necessary medication
- ▸ Slip and fall accidents
- ▸ Staff assaults on patients
- ▸ Patient on patient assaults
- ▸ Infections from unsanitary conditions
- ▸ Sexual abuse

### Survivor's Narrative

I really had no idea how big and powerful the Rehab Industry was until I read what Steve wrote. Having said that, I always assumed Rehabs were regulated in some sort of way—like the rest of the medical industry. I understand now, that's not the case. I was naïve. Like the majority of people.

As far as Rehab's high-priced lawyers and privacy laws being manipulated that Steve speaks about, I had first hand experiences with both issues. I dealt with my Rehab's well-known pricy legal firm that was hired to manipulate my privacy rights to the Rehab's advantage. This firm instigated a law suit against me in the hopes to keep me quiet about my experience in the Rehab and go away. I found out from Steve's attorney the type of lawsuit filed against me was called a "Strategic Lawsuit Against Public Participation" (SLAPP). It's a lawsuit that is intended to censor, intimidate, and silence critics by burdening them with the cost of a legal defense until they abandon their criticism and/or opposition.

Yes, I was very intimidated and scared about being sued because the Rehab asked for a huge financial judgment and attorney fees. After a few weeks the shock wore off of being sued, I got angry. I thought, I almost died in the Rehab, and they are suing me? What? Pretty crazy, huh? But let me regress. Prior to the lawsuit being filed against me, I tried for several months without results to obtain my medical records from the Rehab. I wanted—needed—to see what actually happened to me in their facility. I finally received a registered package. Enclosed in it was a letter from a lawyer placed on top of some of my partial and incomplete medical records.

In the letter the lawyer said some of my medical records he deemed were the Rehabs personal property, and he was withholding them. The Rehab's lawyer had looked at my private medical and records and determined what I should receive. The partial records he did send, I later found out were very incriminating and helpful in winning my countersuit.

Also, in the letter I am called a liar several times, told I will be sued for damages and attorney fees (which ultimately, I was) if I contacted any state and/or federal agencies in regards to the Rehab's services rendered...or start a social media campaign about to warn others about the Rehab.

I was shocked by all this. By sending my complete medical records to their attorney, I felt the Rehab violated my personal privacy and HIPPA[1] rights. On top of that, the attorney, by having all my records had a clear advantage in any legal actions against me. The letter was just the start of my legal conflict with the Rehab. Because of my legal settlement, to this day I have never received the rest of my medical records.

I often wonder. If the documents the lawyer sent me were incriminating and helped me win my case, what the *Hell* did the documents he withheld from me show?

# References

## 14,000 Rehabs

Horvath, G. (Producer), & Finberg, A. (Director). (2016). The business of recovery [Documentary]. USA: Distribber.

National Institute on Drug Abuse. (2018). Drug addiction treatment in the United States. Retrieved from https://www.drugabuse.gov/publications/principles-drug-addiction-treatment-research-based-guide-third-edition/drug-addiction-treatment-in-united-states

---

1 **HIPAA:** Acronym that stands for the Health Insurance Portability and Accountability Act, a US law designed to provide privacy standards to protect patients' medical records.

## The Wild, Wild West

Horvath, G. (Producer), & Finberg, A. (Director). (2016). The business of recovery [Documentary]. USA: Distribber.

Saavedra, T. (2018). Death in rehab generates $7 million award. Retrieved from https://www.ocregister.com/2018/02/08/death-in-rehab-generates-7-million-award/

## Problems in the Rehab industry

Saavedra, T. (2018). Florida prosecutor Dave Aronberg sees parallels in rogue rehabs in Florida and Southern California. Retrieved from https://www.ocregister.com/2018/03/27/florida-prosecutor-dave-aronberg-sees-parallels-in-rogue-rehabs-in-florida-and-southern-california/

Sforza, T. (2018). Sober living, Day 4: Lawmakers must force industry to shape up, many say. Retrieved from https://www.ocregister.com/2018/07/27/sober-living-day-4-lawmakers-must-force-industry-to-shape-up-many-say/

Sforza, T., Saavedra, T., Schwebke, S., Basheda, L., Schauer, M., Gritchen, J., & Wheeler, I. (2018). How some Southern California drug rehab centers exploit addiction. Retrieved from https://www.ocregister.com/2017/05/21/how-some-southern-california-drug-rehab-centers-exploit-addiction/#part1

## SLAPP lawsuit

Wikipedia: The Free Encyclopedia. (2018). Strategic lawsuit against public participation. Retrieved from (https://en.wikipedia.org/wiki/Strategic_lawsuit_against_public_participation

## HIPPA

Villa, L. (2018). Understanding confidentiality and privacy guidelines for treatment centers. Retrieved from https://www.projectknow.com/research/confidentiality-and-privacy/

## CHAPTER TWENTY-TWO

# TOXIC REHAB FEES

Rehabs fully understand they are dealing with people who are vulnerable, sick, who have hit rock bottom and desperately need help. It is a life or death situation. These people at rock bottom place their trust and hope that they will become well in the hands of the Rehabs. In this trusting state, they usually do not question the Rehab's fees. The Rehab is going to save them, and that's what it costs to be saved.

Parents spend their life savings or mortgage their houses (in some cases with help of the Rehab) to pay the fees of a Rehab to save a loved one. They are in the same loop. They have trust and hope the Rehab will save their loved one's life. All they need to do is just get the money the Rehab requires for this to happen.

**Fees**

What are the costs we're talking about that the Rehabs charge to save people? The cost for a stay of 30 days can range from $25,000 to $60,000 a month in the USA, depending on the amenities the Rehab offers for the patient. Some amenities could be high-end spa accommodations, beach locations, horseback riding, and golf. Unfortunately, the amount spent does not increase your chances for sobriety.

The average cost of a stay in a Rehab is $30,000 for 30 days. The documentary *The Business of Recovery*[1] compares this fee to a good senior home that only costs around $4,000 a month. It breaks down the services both offer for their fees and then questions the reasons for the high profit margins of the Rehabs when compared with services of a senior home. It is very revealing and compelling what the documentary lays out. Basically, their premise is you get about the same services at both, but with senior care you get to select your meal choices. Most of the time Rehabs serve cafeteria style food.

**90%**

It has been estimated that 90% of Rehabs base their recovery treatment program fully or partially on the Alcoholics Anonymous (AA) fellowship 12-step program which is non-evidence[2] based and free. In fact, most of the AA literature is free (although

1    Expose Documentary of Rehab Industry produced in 2015.
2    Read Chapter 30, Non-Evidence based treatment.

supported by donations). These Rehabs either have the free meetings in their facility, take the patients to outside meetings, or a combination of both. Rehabs make enormous profits utilizing the free fellowship of AA as the basis of their treatment plan.

## Useless Lectures

Most Rehabs have lectures built into their AA recovery program. William Miller, an expert on addiction, states, "Many of the programs and educational lectures provided by Rehabs have very little, if any, impact on alcohol and substance abuse users; yet clients are being charged thousands of dollars to attend despite the lack of evidence that they have any effect whatsoever." Rehabs should give options on attending lectures to lower costs." I think that idea has merit.

## Repeat Customer

There never has been an industry that makes so much money on a repeat customer. I am not saying Rehabs want patients to relapse, but it is big money when they do. The Rehabs know that, statistically, most patients will relapse many times. In fact, studies show the AA program on which the majority of Rehabs base their recovery program is only 5% to 10% effective—high fees to charge for such a low rate of success.

## Survivor's Narrative

The Rehab I decided on was a basic, no spa, no beach view, no horses, no golf or upscale amenities. The food would be cafeteria style and my bedroom had two beds, one for another patient, one bathroom, no TV.

My wife and I were told a minimum ten-day stay for me to survive cessation of my prescription drug was required. This meant the fee was $10,000.00. The Rehab did a dog-and-pony show taking copies of my insurance card, calling the insurance company in front of me, and promising all was handled. They told me, "Do not worry." I would pay a very minimum from what they were told by the insurance company.

It was agreed there would be a $7,000 charge on my credit card—a deposit to get me in the door. The Rehab would bill my insurance company. It was further agreed the Rehab would not run the $7,000 charge through on the card. That is, until they spoke to me first with the exact amount after they determined what was needed for my stay. The deposit would be then adjusted and processed and sent to my credit card company for collection.

### Overcharged

I was shocked three weeks after I was discharged to discover my credit card had been charged the total $7,000 on the day of my admission. I assumed all was okay financially with the Rehab. I was never consulted on any charges as we agreed. Most importantly, I should have been charged only $3,000, not $7000 for my three days stay in Rehab even if the insurance company turned down all my claims.

Upon contacting my insurance company, I discovered the Rehab never filed any claims on my behalf. I was told it was standard for Rehabs to file claims under all circumstances. This gives a patient a way to appeal if all or some claims are turned down. I was told at the minimum my blood work, EKG, etc. should be paid.

I was further informed by the insurance company the Rehab must file a claim on my behalf for them to send any reimbursement. To this day, the Rehab has refused to send any claims to my insurance company as agreed for reimbursement. Their intentions since day one was to make me a self-pay and not even bother to help me collect from the insurance company. That check-in day was the beginning of my many Toxic Rehab experiences.

### *Keeping the Money*

Upon seeing the charge on my credit card bill, I immediately called the credit card company to initiate a dispute. Paperwork was needed to supported the dispute. However, the problem was the Rehab never gave me any paperwork before entering Rehab, during Rehab, or when discharged in spite of asking for it each time. Each time I was told it would be mailed. Never happened.

With this dispute, the Rehab stated to the credit card company that the $7,000 charge was legitimate for a seven-day stay with them, despite knowing I was there only three days.

The Rehab knew that I did not have any of my financial agreements or discharge papers to offset their statement. I lost this first dispute.

To make a long story short, over six months of many new disputes filed over the same issue, I ultimately won. I finally received copies of my partial records which proved all my statements. The card company had no choice but to rule in my favor with the evidence I sent. My first victory against the Rehab, and I thought it was all over. I was wrong. Losing just infuriated the Toxic Rehab even more.

# Reference

### Rehabs deal with the vulnerable

Horvath, G. (Producer), & Finberg, A. (Director). (2016). The business of recovery [Documentary]. USA: Distribber.

### Costs of Rehabs

Bader, E. J. (2015). "The business of recovery": Putting profits over people hurts public health. Retrieved from https://truthout.org/articles/the-business-of-recovery-putting-profits-over-people-hurts-public-health/

Glaser, G. (2015). The billion-dollar rehab racket that drains family savings. Retrieved from https://www.thedailybeast.com/the-billion-dollar-rehab-racket-that-drains-family-savings

Horvath, G. (Producer), & Finberg, A. (Director). (2016). The business of recovery [Documentary]. USA: Distribber.

Leong, M. (2014). A price tag on life: Rehab for drug and alcohol addiction can be financially damaging. Retrieved from http://business.financialpost. com/personal-finance/a-price-tag-on-life-rehab-for-drug-and-alcohol-addiction-can-be-financially-damaging

Sforza, T. (2018). Addiction treatment: The new gold rush. 'It's almost chic'. Retrieved from https://www.ocregister.com/2017/06/16/addiction-treatment-the-new-gold-rush-its-almost-chic/

## 90% Rehabs use AA

Horvath, G. (Producer), & Finberg, A. (Director). (2016). The business of recovery [Documentary]. USA: Distribber.

## Lectures in Rehabs, ineffective

Horvath, G. (Producer), & Finberg, A. (Director). (2016). The business of recovery [Documentary]. USA: Distribber.

## Rehab recovery program 5% to 10% effective

Glaser, G. (2015). The irrationality of Alcoholics Anonymous. Retrieved from https://www.theatlantic.com/magazine/archive/2015/04/the-irrationality-of-alcoholics-anonymous/386255/

Munro, D. (2015). Inside the $35 billion addiction treatment industry. Retrieved from https://www.forbes.com/sites/danmunro/2015/04/27/inside-the-35-billion-addiction-treatment-industry/#798fc55017dc

Szalavitz, M. (2016). The rehab industry needs to clean up its act. Here's how. Retrieved from https://www.huffingtonpost.com/the-influence/the-rehab-industry-needs-clean-up_b_9210542.html

# TOXIC NON-EMPLOYEE TRAINING

One of the major issues that has caused problems with a patient's unsuccessful recovery or even injury or death in Rehabs, has been the lack of key support staff. This includes qualified addiction counselors. With this lack of trained employees, patients can become victims of staff incompetence and inexperience during their stay in Rehab. What compounds this, untrained employees are not able to make the correct decisions and take the right actions during a medical emergency—which can and does lead to many tragedies in Rehabs.

## Hiring Practices

The trend of management at many Rehabs is to hire people in the progress of recovery themselves for addiction counselors or support staff, which can mean many jobs. Being in recovery appears to be the predominant qualification for hiring.

Going through recovery is not bad in itself, if the person is fully educated and trained to fill the position of an addiction counselor. If not, then he or she should only be hired to offer support with personal successful sobriety stories, lead group meetings, and other work that is non-medical. As for support staff, more often than not, they take on specialized roles without the proper training or education.

Rehabs like to hire recovering addicts because they do not need to offer competitive pay packages. Recovering addicts often find it difficult to obtain employment, and they agree to work at minimum or low-pay salaries. At times they even volunteer their work as interns in exchange for a promise of a paying job in the future or in trade for some benefits the Rehabs have to offer. To add to this troubling employee equation, with a goal to maximize insurance payments, Rehabs will lower operating costs, which usually means understaffing. In addition, some Rehabs do not carry out the necessary background checks on their potential employees, which can lead to all types of problems with patients' health and security.

## Addiction Counselors Training?

Rehabs' requirements for hiring addiction counselors is a mixed bag at the best, due to the Industry not being fully regulated. Some Rehabs do not require their employees to have a specialized education or training before becoming addiction counselors. The only requirement, as mentioned before, is they should be a recovering addict with a minimum of six-months sobriety. These under-educated and under-trained counselors give crucial advice and guidance. Their advice and guidance can have major consequences for a patient's recovery or, for that matter, their patient's life.

At this time in the USA, there is no mandatory national certification exam for addiction counselors. A few states now are requiring addiction counselors to have a BA degree to work in Rehabs. To be more specific, at this time only six states require addiction counselors to have a minimum bachelor's degree and only one state requires a master's degree. Other states have no license requirements at all and some to be credentialed just require only a high school diploma or a GED.

Some self-governed commissions offer voluntary certification programs for addiction counselor training, for example, National Association for Alcoholism and Drug Abuse Counselors (NAA-DAC). Addiction counselor training offered by any commission is strictly voluntary. To be fair, some Rehabs do encourage their counselors to study and obtain at least the basic credentials which is a Credentialed Alcoholism and Substance Abuse Counselor (CASAC). A CASAC requires a high school degree or a GED certificate.

Other titles and credentials you can look for behind an addiction counselor's name to insure he or she has some training include: National Certified Addition Counselor (NCAC) I certificate, NCAC II certificate, Master Addiction Counselor (MAC) certificate, Nicotine Dependence Specialist (NDS) certificate, National Certified Adolescent Addictions Counselor (NCAAC) certificate, and National Certified Peer Recovery Support Specialist (NCPRSS) certificate.

## Survivor's Narrative

My experiences with the Rehab employees was not the best. The main issues were lack of supervision and jobs not being done correctly. When my medical records (the partial records I did receive) were examined, it was discovered the doctor's key elements in my directives and plan for my treatment were not followed. It was ordered I was to be checked on and assessed every two hours at night for seven nights by a nurse for my safety. The four nights I stayed, the nursing charts show I was checked only once a night and my vitals were taken only once during those four times. Now, I was in dire need of some observation and help from a nurse the second night there, as you will find out why later on in Chapter 25 *Toxic Rehab Deaths*.

### I'm a Female?

In my medical reports they referred to me back and forth as a "male or female" which might seem harmless enough on the surface. But an employee sent my labs in for testing and failed to specify my gender. The lab tested all my lab work as a female. Hence, all the results were for a female.

At the top of each of the four pages in bold on my lab results, it states "gender was not submitted" so "female" was used for tests. It is also mentioned that some tests could not be performed because of the doubt regarding gender. Plus, at the top of the lab reports, on each page, is a red flag warning of possible corrupt results. I know now, not one employee—doctor or nurse—ever noticed or read these warnings and red flags on my lab reports. If they did, they neglected to have them redone for accurate results.

These non-performed tests mentioned in the lab reports, you will find out in the next few paragraphs, can be very crucial to a person in Rehab. In fact, the results of female testing would be wrong in ascertaining health issues for a male since different parameters for males and females are used in results of tests for a diagnosis.

## Health Dangers with Corrupt Labs

There is a big difference on some specific lab reports between male and female that can result in a wrong diagnosis and/or prescribed medication if a gender is not correctly specified. For instance, on my corrupt lab reports, my creatinine results were in question because of no indication of gender. Subsequently, the lab refused to do a Glomerular Filtration Rate (GFR) test with the skewed creatine test.

A GFR test measures your level of kidney function and determines if any kidney disease is present and, if so, the stages of the disease. The GFR is calculated from the results of a blood creatinine test, gender, and age. If your GFR number is low, your kidneys are not working as well as they should. The earlier kidney disease is detected, the better the chance of slowing or stopping its progression. This is an important test for patients to have in Rehabs to see if any kidney damage took place from drinking and taking drugs.

## Mixed up Reports

I mentioned my medical reports varied with gender in them. The RN who reviewed my records gave a reason why. She states, "Most likely the reason your doctor reports reflected mixed genders is because he might have gotten files mixed up when he was dictating his reports." Now this makes sense to me because the reports have me drinking a fifth of vodka a day, which I never did. I never consumed that amount of alcohol on a daily basis and did not drink vodka. This major discrepancy in my report and other inaccurate information, might explain why the doctor prescribed the deadly off-label drugs that almost killed me as I explain in Chapter 24.

## My Addiction Counselor

I did have an addiction counselor assigned to me. As far as his training, I really don't know, it was moot anyway. He never had the time to meet with me for a session during my brief stay. Although, in the cafeteria he did introduce himself and handed me information on the AA 12 steps he said read. Never saw him again after that.

# Reference

## Non-Employee Training

Held, M. (2018). What does it mean to be certified, licensed, or accredited in the drug and alcohol treatment industry? Retrieved from https://thriveglobal.com/stories/what-does-it-mean-to-be-certified-licensed-or-accredited-in-the-drug-and-alcohol-treatment-industry/

Held, M. (2018). What does it mean to be certified, licensed, or accredited in the drug and alcohol treatment industry? And why you should care. Retrieved from https://thriveglobal.com/stories/what-does-it-mean-to-be-certified-licensed-or-accredited-in-the-drug-and-alcohol-treatment-industry

Sforz, T., & Saavedra, T. (2018). Legislators taking aim at scams in the drug rehab industry. Retrieved from https://www.ocregister.com/2018/04/24/legislators-taking-aim-at-scams-in-the-drug-rehab-industry/

Staff Report, *The Orange County Register*. (2017). The Southern California rehab industry spans the nation. Retrieved from https://www.ocregister.com/2017/05/21/the-southern-california-rehab-industry-spans-the-nation/

## Rehab Hiring Practices

Lanzone Morgan LLP. (2018). Problems with drug rehab centers. Retrieved from http://www.lanzonemorgan.com/drug-rehab-center-abuse-cases/problems-with-drug-rehab-centers/

Munro, D. (2015). Inside the $35 billion addiction treatment industry. Retrieved from https://www.forbes.com/sites/danmunro/2015/04/27/inside-the-35-billion-addiction-treatment-industry/#4811dbcf17dc

Sforza, T., & Saavedra, T. (2018). Quest for sobriety often ends in sexual assault at some rehabs in Southern California. Retrieved from https://www.ocregister.com/2018/01/19/quest-for-sobriety-often-ends-in-sexual-assault-at-some-rehabs-in-southern-california/

# Chapter Twenty-Three: Toxic Non-Employee Training

Staff Report, *The Orange County Register*. (2017). The Southern California rehab industry spans the nation. Retrieved from https://www.ocregister.com/2017/05/21/the-southern-california-rehab-industry-spans-the-nation/

Szalavitz, M. (2013). Q & A: What really goes on in drug rehabs. Retrieved from http://healthland.time.com/2013/02/15/qa-what-really-goes-on-in-drug-rehabs/

# CHAPTER TWENTY-FOUR

# TOXIC OFF-LABEL DRUGS

Prescription drugs when prescribed for other uses (this includes different dosages) than what is approved by the FDA are called off-labeled drugs. The main risk posed by the use of off-label drugs is that they are more likely to increase the risk of adverse effects or even life-threating situations. The simple reason being the drugs are not being used for what they were made for, and this use has not been safety tested.

Off-label drugs are used in Rehabs for the treatment of withdrawal symptoms, sleep issues, emotional issues, etc. It is up to the Rehab doctor to prescribe a drug and the protocol for it. The problem is a Rehab doctor will prescribe drugs off-label on the advice of the manufacturer who will fund independent studies. The studies tell the possibilities of what the off-label drug can be taken for, but not what the FDA will approve it for.

## Kickbacks

What is really troubling about off-label drugs is their manufacturers spend millions and millions of dollars marketing and promoting them to doctors to prescribe. In some cases, kickbacks are given to doctors for writing those prescriptions. The USA government has sued many drug manufacturers for this practice. Over $13 billion in fines have been paid by major drug companies to settle lawsuits against them for their fraudulent marketing practices. This includes off-label promotion of their drugs. Here are just a few cases of many settled lawsuits:

- Parke-Davis, Warner-Lambert and Pfizer (again) in 2004 agreed to pay $430 million to resolve all civil and criminal liability for the off-label promotion of Neurontin.
- In 2009, Pfizer (again) agreed to pay $2.3 billion to settle allegations of kickbacks in an off-label marketing campaign for various drugs.

There is a reason I list the settlement for the drug Neurontin. Neurontin is an approved epilepsy drug that was promoted for other uses. This drug is still being used off-label in some Rehabs. Survivor's narrative will give the details.

## Laundry List

Upon entering a Rehab, patients sign a laundry list of the drugs they will be prescribed. Then (maybe) they are asked if they have any questions about the drugs on the list. Of course not! Patients don't have a clue what to ask and are already under the influence of the Rehab's meds or what they took or drank before they got there. At this vulnerable point, they trust the Rehab doctor and assume all the drugs they will be given are approved by the FDA for the reasons they are taking them.

Let me expand on the above point. When you pick up a new prescription at a pharmacy, they always ask if you want to talk to the pharmacist about the dosage, side effects, etc., of the drug. Not in Toxic Rehabs. They just want your signature on the list in case you have problems with the drugs, so they can say you were fully informed before you were administered the drug.

## Survivor's Narrative

I was over-medicated and almost died because I was pre-scribed two heavy-duty, off-label drugs without fully explaining to me what I was being given and the side effects of such drugs. If my wife and I had been fully informed about these drugs, under no circumstances would I have taken them. Who would?

I was given a list of drugs being prescribed and was told everybody receives them the first week in Rehab and asked if I had any questions. "Anything I should know about the drugs that can harm me?" The nurse said, "Of course not."

If you're going into a Rehab, read the segment, "Selecting a Non-Toxic Rehab." If I had had this knowledge, it would have saved me going through my horrible Rehab nightmare.

## *The Drugs*

The two off-label drugs prescribed for me were Trileptal[1] and Neurontin[2], both normally used cautiously for epileptics on-label. I can only presume the drugs should be prescribed as a last resort for people with high chances of brutal withdrawal. I was not in that category. If you look at the side effects for these drugs on-label they mirror withdrawal effects. Anyway, my Rehab charts showed the afternoon I checked into Rehab I had one chance of withdrawal symptoms and the next morning they assessed me at zero chance for withdrawal symptoms. Another note added to my withdrawal chart read, "Overall mental, physical, health excellent. Appearance, memory, speech, reflexes good." Nonetheless, in spite of the just about non-existent chances of my having any major withdrawal symptoms, the Rehab still gave me the high-risk, off-label drug duo.

Even after the Rehab settled with me, I never received an explanation about why these two drugs were prescribed to me. I do not know if giving the drugs were just a mistake because nobody read my charts, or they mixed up my charts with a female vodka-drinking patient[3] in Rehab at the same time I was.

In the next chapter, "Toxic Rehab Deaths," I will describe my near-death experience with off-label drugs in Rehab.

---

1    An anticonvulsant drug used primarily in the treatment of epilepsy.
2    A drug used to control partial seizures in adults with epilepsy.
3    I mentioned this possibility in Chapter 23 in my narrative.

# References

## Off-label drugs

Miller, K. (2009). Off-label drug use: What you need to know. Retrieved from https://www.webmd.com/a-to-z-guides/features/off-label-drug-use-what-you-need-to-know#1

U.S. Food & Drug Administration. (2018). Understanding unapproved use of approved drugs "Off Label." Retrieved from https://www.fda.gov/ForPatients/Other/OffLabel/default.htm

Ventola, C. L. (2009). Off-label drug information: Regulation, distribution, evaluation, and related controversies. Retrieved from https://www.ncbi.nlm.nih.gov/pmc/articles/PMC2799128/

## Drug kickbacks convictions

Department of Law: State of Georgia. (2009). Pfizer to pay $2.3 billion to settle allegations of kickbacks in off-label marketing campaign. Retrieved from https://law.georgia.gov/press-releases/2009-09-02/pfizer-pay-23-billion-settle-allegations-kickbacks-label-marketing

Harris, G. (2004). Pfizer to pay $430 million over promoting drug to doctors. Retrieved from https://www.nytimes.com/2004/05/14/business/pfizer-to-pay-430-million-over-promoting-drug-to-doctors.html

# CHAPTER TWENTY-FIVE

# TOXIC REHAB DEATHS

Most deaths and injuries in Rehabs are not reported for many reasons. They are covered up by the Rehab, confidential legal settlements, and court-sealed documents—to name a few. It behooves Rehabs to keep deaths under wraps so as not to impact business. What this means most of the time is the loved ones of the victim never really find out what actually happened. Or, at best, they receive a convoluted, ambiguous story of the events that led to the victim's death.

The most flagrant deaths are investigated by the state agencies and make the six o'clock news. This is usually because of the victim family's outcry. The outcomes of these lengthy investigations and court battles usually never make it on the news or are reported in a much smaller news segment.

Most states and the USA Federal Government do not keep statics of deaths and injuries in Rehabs. I did find a report on Rehab death statistics in California. It was an NBC investigative report. It stated a patient dies in a California Rehab facility every two weeks. When the NBC statistics are extrapolated to other states, the death numbers can be shocking.

## Survivor's Narrative

I almost became a Rehab death statistic because I was pre-scribed two off-label drugs, the two drugs I wrote about in the previous chapter, "Off-Label Drugs." Before I tell details of the story that happened to me, I want to add this. The nurse who reviewed my medical records and heard my story said most likely I had had a seizure in my sleep from the off-label drugs prescribed to me. This caused me to lose the use of my legs when I woke up, and I was lucky I stopped taking both drugs. If I hadn't, I could have had a stroke—or worse—died as a result of the continued use of them.

### *My Near-Death Incident*

Early morning of my second night in Rehab, I awoke not being able to move either of my legs. They were numb, paralyzed. There was no way to contact the nurse's desk about this chilling predicament I was in. I did not have a nurse-call button. Realizing I was on my own, instinctively I decided what to do. I rolled out of bed onto the floor and, with my upper body strength,

I crawled, dragging my legs behind me into the bathroom shower stall. Once in, I was able to reach the hot water knob. I ran hot water on my legs, massaging them back and forth for many, many hours. Thank God! Finally, I was able to pull myself up slowly and was able to hobble to the nurse's station.

Entering the morning nurse's station, I told the nurse what had happened to me. The nurse started taking fast notes of my story, but she was silent, her face grim. I asked her what had happened to me. She had no idea—really did not know, not a clue. Once again, I relied on my instincts and asked what medications were being given to me. She read a list of drugs and the two off-label drugs were on it, although at the time I didn't know what they were or their significance to what had happened to me.

I decided for my health and wellbeing I would stop taking all drugs they were giving me right then and there. That was one of the best decisions I've ever made in my life. Throughout the rest of my Rehab stay, the nursing staff tried to give me the cocktail list of drugs ordered for me by the Rehab doctor.

The rest of that day, I told my story to all medical staff I encountered and asked for guidance on what happened to me. I just wanted to alleviate my fears that my legs would not become permanently paralyzed. Everyone I spoke to acted like I had the plague and stonewalled me about my inquiries. It seemed to me all medical staff were closing ranks and not talking to me about my situation. After my legal battle with the Rehab, I know that was true.

### *Kicked Out*

That evening I was suddenly told that I was being discharged early the next morning. I was shocked and depressed and worried at this turn of events. As you remember, at the start of Rehab, my wife and I were told I would most likely need more than 10 days in Rehab to survive. Now, all of a sudden, I was being discharged seven days early. I was offered the opportunity to call my wife that night, but I refused it until the morning. I knew she would be distraught at the turn of the events. She was.

The morning of my discharge, a disturbing thing happened to me. I met with a Rehab doctor for my discharge papers. He promptly handed me a 10-day prescription for the anti-seizure drug Trileptal. I was speechless. I could only assume the medical staff had not fully charted and taken any notes of the incident with my legs, and my subsequent refusal to take any drugs, including Trileptal. So, with this assumption the doctor was not aware of this—or even more disturbing— the Dr. was aware of my problems and concerns with Trileptal, but gave the prescription anyway. I did not fill the prescription.

A major side note on this narrative. Once I stopped taking the two off-label drugs, what I experienced with my legs never happened to me again.

# References

## Rehab deaths

Alltucker, K. (2017). What happened? Family seeks answers after Ohio woman, 22, dies during Arizona rehab stint. Retrieved from https://www.azcentral.com/story/news/local/arizona-investigations/2017/10/18/what-happened-family-seeks-answers-after-ohio-woman-22-dies-during-arizona-rehab-stint/772715001/

Henry, J. (2018). State shuts down Pasadena-based 'Celebrity Rehab' center over death, repeated violations. Retrieved from https://www.ocregister.com/2018/08/04/state-shuts-down-pasadena-based-celebrity-rehab-center-over-death-repeated-violations/

Nguyen, V., Campos, R., Rutanooshedech, A., & Carroll, J. (2018). NBC Bay Area investigation reveals rehab centers' complaint and death records difficult to track. Retrieved from https://www.nbcbayarea.com/news/local/NBC-Bay-Area-Investigation-Reveals-Rehab-Centers-Complaint-and-Death-Records-Difficult-to-Track-475614053.html

Saavedra, T., & Sforza, T. (2018). Death in rehab generates $7 million award. Retrieved from https://www.ocregister.com/2018/02/08/death-in-rehab-generates-7-million-award/

Sforza, T. (2017). Detox can end in death at some 'non-medical' Southern California rehabs. Retrieved from https://www.ocregister.com/2017/12/17/detox-can-end-in-death-at-some-non-medical-southern-california-rehabs

Snibbe, K. (2017). Where and how much deadly addictions have consumed America. Retrieved from https://www.ocregister.com/2017/05/22/where-and-how-much-deadly-addictions-have-consumed-america/

Staff Report, *The Orange County Register*. (2017). The Southern California rehab industry spans the nation. Retrieved from https://www.ocregister.com/2017/05/21/the-southern-california-rehab-industry-spans-the-nation/

# CHAPTER TWENTY-SIX

# TOXIC SOBER HOUSES

Step sisters of the Rehab Industry are called "Sober Houses." Sober Houses are supposed to provide alcohol- and drug-free living environments. That's not always the case. Most are also based on the AA 12-step program (same as Rehabs) and the houses are for individuals attempting to maintain abstinence. The cost of a stay in a Sober House is 50% to 75% less than a Rehab.

**Sober Houses Facts**

Sober Houses are privately owned and cannot legally provide or engage in any sort of medical service. The challenge is that almost anyone can open a sober house, even the owner of a private residence. It's not necessary for the owner to have any special qualifications, certifications, licensing, or training. It's the same "no requirements" for the under-skilled staff hired at low wages who take care of the people who stay in them; therefore, the property owners can easily make huge profits on their operations.

Sober Houses provide virtually no supervision, social services, drug or alcohol treatment programs, security or rehabilitation. Unfortunately, this creates a breeding ground for violence, drug use, and overdoses. They recruit paying customers by stating they provide counseling which is usually AA meetings. Some blatantly tell gullible prospective patients they are like Rehabs but with much lower fees. Sober Houses have been known to house recovering addicts in unsafe and small quarters, risking their recovery, health and safety.

If a Sober House is run properly, ethically, and legally it can be a viable option for certain people, but buyer beware.

### Survivor's Narrative

My first attempt at recovery was about three years prior to my Toxic Rehab experience. I know now what I checked into for help was a Sober House. At the time, I thought all places offering recovery treatment programs were Rehabs, and all were basically the same. Boy, was I was so wrong. Anyway, I wound up in this Sober House because it was about 75% cheaper than other Rehabs I'd contacted.

## *My Stay*

I stayed in the Sober House with about twelve other people. In the house, there were not really any trained professional employees that I could detect. There were a few volunteers around who said they were recovering alcoholics to keep law and order. For food, it was cooking on your own whatever was in the refrigerator.

Recovery treatment consisted of AA meetings held daily in the house and every other day we were bussed to one. Drugs being used by some people in the house, but I was never offered any, or asked for any.

A nurse assistant would come by on a daily basis to give meds to patients. Meds were prescribed by a person I assumed was a doctor whom I met in the main office before I was taken to the Sober House. It's embarrassing to say with what I know now, but I do not know what they were giving me. The meds did give me a great high.

## *Whose Pills Are These?*

On the fourth day, the nurse (I was told she was a nurse) who handed out medications at five p.m. every day didn't show. Two of the volunteers on duty found the meds and started to hand out them out. The problem was all the meds were in small packages, without names or labels. The volunteers started opening the packets and asking each of us, "Is this your medication? If so, how much do you take?" Was this really happening?

Every pill looked similar to me and all I really knew was that I was taking five pills. At this point I was very concerned about this Mickey Mouse (sorry Walt!) operation and wanted to get out of there ASAP. There were a few problems with that. I didn't know where I was and my wallet, money, cards, and ID were confiscated from me before I was taken to the Sober House.

While they were still figuring out who got what meds, I left the house and walked down the street to see where the heck I was. That didn't help, I was still lost. I walked back to the house. I started to enter, but a volunteer blocked my entry. He told me I couldn't come back in because I'd left the premises without his permission. Really? I don't recall being told that rule.

I told him that and that I would leave and go home, except my wallet was at the main office, so I couldn't call Uber for a ride home. And my belongings were in the house. That didn't sway him. He said something to the effect that I have to learn the hard way like he did. Thinking quickly. I told him I'd go knock on the neighbor's door and ask to use a phone to call the police and tell them my situation. In my story to the police, I would include that he was handing out prescribed medications without a license to many people. Bingo, that did it. I was told to wait on the porch while he made a phone call to the Sober House's CEO. About 60 minutes later I was personally driven home with all my belongings.

### *Aftermath*

I did meet with the CEO a few days later and he said what happened at the house with the meds and the way I was treated was a fluke. All caused by a bad volunteer who had since been terminated. He offered to refund my money for the few days I stayed in the house and assured me that would never happen again to another patient. I accepted his offer and soon forgot about this short-lived incident, and kept taking my prescribed Valium. After reading Steve's chapter on Sober Houses, the one I landed up in seems like the cream of the crop of Sober Houses.

# References

## Sober Houses crack downs

Harmonson, T. (2017). O.C. district attorney charges family, doctors with insurance fraud related to sober living homes, urine tests. Retrieved from https://www.ocregister.com/2017/05/23/o-c-district-attorney-charges-family-doctors-with-insurance-fraud-related-to-sober-living-homes-urine-tests/

Kath, R. (2017). Mother of opioid overdose victim warns of unregulated sober houses. Retrieved from http://boston.cbslocal.com/2017/09/19/mother-of-opioid-overdose-victim-warns-of-unregulated-sober-houses/

Partnership News Service Staff. (2013). Unregulated "sober homes" often provide poor living conditions. Retrieved from shttps://drugfree.org/learn/drug-and-alcohol-news/unregulated-sober-homes-often-provide-poor-living-conditions/

Saavedra, T. (2017). Rehab mogul will stand trial in $176 million fraud case. Retrieved from https://www.ocregister.com/2017/05/09/rehab-mogul-will-stand-trial-in-176-million-fraud-case/

Samuel, L. (2016). As opioid epidemic spikes, states crack down on 'sober homes'. Retrieved from https://www.statnews.com/2016/05/10/sober-homes-state-crackdown

Sforza, T. (2018). Empower local governments to regulate wayward sober homes, witnesses tell Congress. Retrieved from https://www.ocregister.com/2018/09/28/empower-local-governments-to-regulate-wayward-sober-homes-witnesses-tell-congress/

Sforza, T., & Saavedra, T. (2018). Huntington Beach, Orange County team up to sue sober homes. Retrieved from https://www.ocregister.com/2018/10/19/huntington-beach-orange-county-team-up-to-sue-sober-homes/

# CHAPTER TWENTY-SEVEN

# TOXIC GOOGLE

In a study, Google found 61% of the people in Rehabs, found them Online. Therein lies the problem—questionable, deceptive, and dog-eat-dog marketing by Rehabs searching for the 61% on-line dollars. This type of marketing got so out of hand and created such a barrage of consumer complaints globally, that in 2017, Google finally closed down Rehab advertising on their search engine.

Below are just some of the marketing tactics used that caused the Google shutdown:

- Advertised services and amenities that sometimes were not factual. Rehabs wrote anything on a website with the end game of making prospective patients call their number.
- Rehabs listed themselves and services incorrectly on web sites to quote lower fees. For instance, a Rehab might imply it was a live-in facility, but was actually an outpatient facility.

▸ Websites positioned themselves as objective referral sources with your best interests in mind. In reality they were selling leads to the highest bidding Rehab.

▸ Rehabs created landing pages that were informative, but captured information without permission for their own salespeople.

▸ Some Rehabs had sophisticated programs that actually hijacked Web traffic from other Rehab sites and directed the traffic to their own sites.

**Bottom Line**

The bottom line is this. When you call the toll-free number on a Rehab website, you will be speaking with a salesman, a salesman who receives a substantial commission to sell you a Rehab stay. Think of a Rehab salesperson as a used-car salesman. Both are highly trained and can say pretty much whatever it takes to make the sale. Because they both know they only have one shot to close the deal with you on the phone or on the car lot, or you move on to the next online listing or car lot.

**Google Cracks Down**

Below are highlights from *The Verge* which reported on the beginning of Google's crack down on deceptive online marketing by Rehabs. Their reporting says it all.

The Verge Exclusive: "Google is cracking down on sketchy rehab ads."

> Around the world today, marketers in the multi-billion addiction treatment industry woke up to an unpleasant surprise. Many of their Google search ads were gone. Overnight, the search giant has stopped selling ads against a huge number of rehab-related search terms, including "rehab near me," "alcohol treatment," and thousands of others. Search ads on some of those keywords would previously have netted Google hundreds of dollars per click, worldwide.
>
> "We found a number of misleading experiences among rehabilitation treatment centers that led to our decision, in consultation with experts, to restrict ads in this category," Google told *The Verge* in a statement. "As always, we constantly review our policies to protect our users and provide good experiences for consumers."

**Each Click Big $**

Rehabs tell Google how much they want to spend on search ads per month, which keywords they'd like those ads to run, and then pay Google every time someone clicks on their ad. For example, a pay-per-click ad *Verge* was talking about on Google, used the words in a google search "alcohol rehab near me." This word search can cost a Rehab $230 a click in some markets with the low-end dollar click at $43.00—really big money with 1,000s of clicks a day. This data about clicks cost was compiled by SEMrush[1] in 2017.

---

1    Online site that you can manage your SEO and Advertising Content.

**Has It Changed?**

This announcement came out for Reuters months later after the crack down.

> SAN FRANCISCO (Reuters) Google told Reuters Monday it would resume accepting ads from U.S. addiction treatment centers in July, nearly a year after the Alphabet Inc. (GOOGL.O) unit suspended the lucrative category of advertisers for numerous deceptive and misleading ads.

From my observations it looks like the Rehabs have found loopholes in Google's new policy for vetting Rehab marketing. While researching this book with the new policy in place, I was continually hijacked with my word searches to a few specific Rehabs web sites. I will leave it at that.

### Survivor's Narrative

I did not find my Rehab in a Google search online. I found my Rehab from a referral from a so-called addiction specialist. I later found out though my lawsuit this person is what is commonly called in the Rehab Industry a "Body Broker."

### Body Brokering

Body Brokering is a term associated with "selling" addicts to treatment centers in return for a kickback, aka placement fee. My addiction specialist was a body broker who steered me to the Rehab for a fee. I trusted this person at the time and did not look at other Rehabs. Body Brokering also includes bribing patients with cash, drugs, and other incentives to enter a specific Rehab. Some brokers visit Alcoholics Anonymous meetings to find people they can send to rehab for kickbacks.

The end game for the body broker is the placement fee from the Rehab. According to an investigation by Phoenix 3TV/CBS 5, body brokers can make anywhere between $100 to $5,000 per addict. According to one anonymous Body Broker, he could make over $25,000 a month referring people to Rehabs. Body Brokering is an unethical and shady practice of Toxic Rehabs. I personally feel there should be a national law against the practice.

# References

### Google's Rehabs crackdown

Dave, P. (2018). Exclusive: Google unveils vetting process for drug rehab ads. Retrieved from https://www.reuters.com/article/us-alphabet-google-ads-exclusive/exclusive-google-unveils-vetting-process-for-drug-rehab-ads-idUSKBN1HN28X

Ferguson, C. (2017). Exclusive: Google is cracking down on sketchy rehab ads. Retrieved from https://www.theverge.com/2017/9/14/16309752/google-rehabs-near-me-search-adwords-crackdown

Ferguson, C. (2017). Searching for help. Retrieved from https://www.theverge.com/2017/9/7/16257412/rehabs-near-me-google-search-scam-florida-treatment-centers

## Rehabs deceptive web marketing

Sforza, T., & Saavedra, T. (2018). Rehab Riviera: Addiction advertising can trick you to death. Retrieved from https://www.ocregister.com/2018/03/02/rehab-riviera-addiction-advertising-can-trick-you-to-death/

Sforza, T., & Saavedra, T. (2018). Rehab Riviera: Addiction rehab ads will return to Google, but they'll be vetted. Retrieved from https://www.ocregister.com/2018/04/20/rehab-riviera-addiction-rehab-ads-will-return-to-google-but-theyll-be-vetted/

Szalavitz, M. (2017). The rehab industry needs to clean up its act. Here's how. Retrieved from https://www.huffingtonpost.com/the-influence/the-rehab-industry-needs-clean-up_b_9210542.html

## Body Brokering

Carise, D. (2017). Some addiction treatment practices are making me sick. Retrieved from https://www.huffingtonpost.com/entry/some-addiction-treatment-practices-are-making-me-sick_us_58c19d97e4b070e55af9ec7d

Sforza, T., & Saavedra, T. (2017). Rehab patient brokering is rampant, but it's hard to stop, industry says. Retrieved from https://www.ocregister.com/2017/05/30/rehab-riviera-in-addiction-industry-even-simple-fixes-are-hard/

Sforza, T., & Saavedra, T. (2018). Legislators taking aim at scams in the drug rehab industry. Retrieved from https://www.ocregister.com/2018/04/24/legislators-taking-aim-at-scams-in-the-drug-rehab-industry/

# CHAPTER TWENTY-EIGHT

# TOXIC INTAKE ASSESSMENTS

A patient is supposed to have an in-depth interview before entering a Rehab. This interview is called an "intake assessment." This assessment is to ascertain where patients are with their addictions past and present, their health (including emotional), issues past and present, if suicidal, if detox is needed and if so, what type of detox and how long. This assessment information determines the treatment and recovery plan for the patient during his or her Rehab stay.

**Valid Assessment**

A valid intake assessment is the difference between success and failure for the patient in Rehab. A faulty one, at a minimum, can mean a difficult recovery or no recovery for the patient. The worst-case assessment can mean death or injury for the patient. Death or injury can occur if it was not determined during the assessment the level of the patient's addiction for withdrawal purposes, or if the patient had other major health issues the Rehab would need to take in account during the patient's stay.

The intake assessment should take several hours at a minimum in a private area and should be conducted by a highly trained, credentialed individual who specializes in this process. The assessment should include multiple interviews including family members if possible, probing questionnaires on addiction, health history current and past, and emotional stability, with review and follow-up questions about the answers. Toxic Rehabs give fast and non-comprehensive assessments usually given by non-qualified personnel.

The main focus with Toxic Rehabs is not the intake assessment, but how long the person can stay and is it paid for. Once they have the days and payment confirmed, it's a rush to get the patient checked in.

### Survivor's Narrative

The Rehab I checked into never had what Steve talks about—a valid intake assessment. I did briefly answer some questions before I entered the Rehab. Even with this, I found out later when I received some of my medical records, most of that information had been put down in my file wrong.

The person asking me questions for my brief assessment was the salesperson for the Rehab. It was apparent he was more interested in getting my credit card, the agreement signed, and getting me into the Rehab ASAP. Once I was in the Rehab, his job was done, commissioned earned.

The Sober House I was in had no assessment of any kind that I recall. A brochure and sales person/counselor took my money, walked me through their basic check in process, then drove me to the Sober House.

# Reference

### Intake assessment

Laplante, C. (2018). What are drug addiction assessments for? Retrieved from https://www.projectknow.com/research/assessment/

Staff Report, Alcohol.org. (2018). The intake process at an alcoholic rehab center. Retrieved from https://www.alcohol.org/rehab-centers/intake/

Staff Report, RehabCenter.net. (2018). What to expect at a substance abuse evaluation. Retrieved from https://www.rehabcenter.net/what-to-expect-at-a-substance-abuse-evaluation/

# CHAPTER TWENTY-NINE

# TOXIC INFORMED CONSENT

Informed consent is the process by which the patients are told about the treatment to be given for their health issue. Informed consent should fully explain all aspects of the treatment, including the benefits and risks. Fully informed, the patient can then decide whether to proceed with the treatment. Here are a few fundamental elements of informed consent:

- ▸ A detailed explanation of the health condition of the patient.
- ▸ The benefits and the risks of the suggested treatment.
- ▸ An explanation of the alternative treatment options.

## Decision-Making Capacity

To give informed consent, a patient must have what is legally termed "decision-making capacity." Decision-making capacity is one of the most important components of informed consent. The key components of decision-making capacity are as follows:

- The ability to understand the option(s) for treatment.
- The ability to understand the consequences of choosing each of the option(s).
- The ability to evaluate the personal cost and benefit of each of the consequences and relate them to your own set of values and priorities.

## The Problems

There are inherent problems with informed consent in Rehabs—the main one being that excessive consumption of alcohol and drugs affects the decision-making capability of a person before he or she checks into a Rehab. The majority of people entering Rehab are under the influence. If they are explained the benefits, risks, and limitations of the treatment, they cannot make an informed consent. They are lacking the ability needed for the decision-making capacity.

The ideal solution for this would to be sober when entering a Rehab. While that is not possible all the time, at least the person should have a friend or relative by his side to assist in the process. Now the challenge is that a Toxic Rehab will keep a person isolated from any help with informed consent. They do this to make sure the person does not have questions and answers that could delay or stop entering the Rehab.

If a person is under the influence and does not have help with informed consent, it's even better for Toxic Rehabs. They do not have to explain anything. They are in complete control of the person without any accountability or explanation of their planned actions.

## Survivor's Narrative

I had no informed consent. Nothing was fully explained to me. It was all a rush to get me to sign the agreement and enter the Rehab. I was constantly told during this process to trust them like the thousands of people who came before for their help...so I trusted them. They did say any questions I have now, save them for later. Later never arrived. My wife had a lot of questions, but they kept her from being with me during the check-in process. I was clueless. I should have demanded that she be there with me at all times, or I would call the deal off. Please, do not make my same mistake. If you are lucky to have a loved one with you during your Rehab check-in, make sure he or she stays by your side to demand informed consent and hear your informed consent. This person will be your canary in the coal mine.

# References

## Informed consent

Staff Report, Dara Thailand. (2018). Informed consent for addiction treatment. Retrieved from https://alcoholrehab.com/drug-addiction-treatment/informed-consent-for-addiction-treatment/

Wagner, R. A. (2018). Informed Consent. Retrieved from https://www.emedicinehealth.com/informed_consent/article_em.htm

# CHAPTER THIRTY

# TOXIC NON-EVIDENCE BASED TREATMENT

Non-evidence Based Treatments (NEBT) are recovery treatment programs that have no real scientific data showing success. The most commonly used NEBT in the majority of Rehabs is the AA 12-step program, a fellowship program.

Here is a quote from Dr. Lance Dodes, a Harvard researcher on the challenges of NEBT programs, specifically the AA NEBT:

> "AA programs are useful for 5%–10%. The problem is that the other 90% of people who are referred to AA—and that is almost everyone with an addiction —are being hurt by being sent to a program that can't possibly help them." Nearly 50% of the general population deals with mental health issues. Most people

with these mental health issues are most likely to also be victims of addiction. There are low success rates when people use non-evidence-based treatments for addiction, and therefore, the number of relapses is on a rise. Non-evidence-based treatments also put patients at risk because of lack of individualized care."

I am not disparaging AA, but if on the high side, statistics claim that only ten percent of AA members are able to obtain sobriety with the program, I ask like Dr. Dodes, what about the remaining 90 percent? With these high numbers is it copacetic for Toxic Rehab Centers to charge millions of dollars on a free NEBT with such a high failure rate? As for the other 90% of the people, I feel confident I have supplied many options for them in this *Resource Guide*.

## Evidence-Based Treatment

Evidence-Based Treatment (EBT) programs are recovery therapies that have been scientifically and medically proven to help people get clean and sober from their alcohol and/or drug addiction. Very few Rehabs use any form of EBT simply because it is expensive—not because it does not work.

One EBT therapy that is commonly used is Cognitive Behavioral Therapy (CBT)[1]. There are different types of CBT. A few are Dialectic Behavior Therapy, Rational Living Therapy, Rational

---

1    Cognitive Behavior Therapy (CBT) is a time-sensitive, structured, present-oriented psychotherapy directed toward solving current problems and teaching skills to modify dysfunctional thinking and behavior.

Behavior Therapy, Cognitive Therapy, and Rational Emotive Behavior Therapy. All of these CBTs are effective for recovery. CBT is usually included in most EBT Rehabs.

## Cheaper

An EBT Rehab is much costlier and more time intensive than operating a NEBT Rehab. An EBT program would require college-educated and degreed professionals to run it. It would also require one-on-one counseling sessions for the patients. Sessions that would be conducted by college-credentialed, addiction specialists. One-on-one professional counseling sessions alone would require far more operating costs. Sessions or group sessions in a NEBT Rehab are usually done by recovering volunteers or employees as described in the Chapter 25 Toxic Employees. As you can see, the costs for NEBT sessions are far less than that of EBT sessions—lot less.

### Survivor's Narrative

The Rehab I was in for recovery was Non-Evidenced Based. Its recovery program was the AA 12 steps. It consisted of in-house and outside 12-step meetings and lectures. They did have voluntary lectures you could attend to supplement their AA program. A few lectures I remember were on Chakra and Reiki Healing.

AA does work for some people. It is up to individuals to be fully informed and make educated decisions about what might work for them. If what they select the first time does not work, there are many other options for recovery. Like Steve, I sincerely feel this *Resource Guide* offers many lifesaving options. Just keep trying until you find one that works for you.

# References

### Non-Evidenced based treatment

Besselink, A. (2011). Is non-evidence-based clinical practice an ethical dilemma? Retrieved from http://www.allanbesselink.com/blog/smart/854-is-non-evidence-based-clinical-practice-an-ethical-dilemma

Horvath, G. (Producer), & Finberg, A. (Director). (2016). The business of recovery [Documentary]. USA: Distribber.

Sindewald, L. (2017). AA is not evidence-based treatment. Retrieved from https://www.thefix.com/aa-is-not-evidence-based-addiction-treatment

Staff Report, Autism Science Foundation. (2018). Beware of non-evidence-based treatments. Retrieved from https://autismsciencefoundation.org/what-is-autism/beware-of-non-evidence-based-treatments/

### Evidenced based treatment

Staff Report, drugrehab.org. (2018). Evidence-based drug rehab centers–the future for addiction treatment. Retrieved from https://www.drugrehab.org/evidence-based-drug-rehab-centers-the-future-for-addiction-treatment/

Staff Report, GoodTherapy. (2016). Evidence-based treatment (EBT). Retrieved from https://www.goodtherapy.org/blog/psychpedia/evidence-based-treatment

Staff Report, National Institute on Drug Abuse. (2018). Evidence-based approaches to drug addiction treatment. Retrieved from https://www.drugabuse.gov/publications/principles-drug-addiction-treatment-research-based-guide-third-edition/evidence-based-approaches-to-drug-addiction-treatment

Wikipedia. (2018). Evidence-based practice. Retrieved from https://en.wikipedia.org/wiki/Evidence-based_practice

# CHAPTER THIRTY-ONE

# SELECTING A NON-TOXIC REHAB

If you decide you need to look into a Rehab, this chapter gives you comprehensive guidance to prevent you from having the same experience as the Survivor had with his Rehab. In other words, it will keep you from selecting a Toxic Rehab.

When going through the steps in this chapter if at any time a Rehab does not fully cooperate with you, a red flag should go up. If that happens, I recommend eliminating the Rehab from your list of options right then. If a Rehab will not cooperate with you before you check in, and there are negative issues during your stay, believe me on this—you will have a major challenge in getting the issue(s) rectified with the Rehab.

Even if your health insurance or government pays for a Rehab stay, or it's a government-sponsored Rehab you are going into as in Canada and the UK, I would still advise you to do as many of the steps as possible. After all, it's your recovery, and your life depends on a successful recovery.

## Rehab 101

There are basically two types of Rehabs. One is inpatient where you stay in the Rehab's facility 24 hours for a certain agreed-to number of days. It can as little as seven days up to 60 days or more. The second one is an outpatient Rehab. Rehab activities take place during the day and you go home at night. This could be a half a day or full day, depending on the Rehab. Some outpatient Rehabs have evening programs to avoid disrupting your employment. A few Rehabs have the option of either inpatient or outpatient treatments.

Both types of Rehabs will have a recovery program based on a specific foundation. The recovery program can be used in conjunction with drugs, vitamins, food, and exercise protocols depending on the Rehab. It's up to you to determine what that is before you make the decision of entering the Rehab. You need to make sure the Rehab you enter is one that resonates with you and is based on your beliefs. If you do not do this, there is a good chance the Rehab's recovery program will not be the most effective for you. Below are the basic foundations of most treatment programs. I spoke about them throughout the *Guide* but will review them again now. This way you will have them for your Rehab interview.

*Secular:* Non-religious based recovery programs. Programs have no religious or spiritual overtones or dogma, although some of these programs might espouse some spiritual philosophy.

*Non-secular:* Spiritual or religious-based recovery programs. These programs are based on religion, such as Christianity, Jewish, Muslim, Hindu, etc.

*12 Steps:* Recovery programs that are based exclusively on the 12 steps of Alcoholics Anonymous[1] and the rest of the Alcoholics Anonymous program.

*Non-12 Step:* Recovery programs that are not based on the 12 steps used in Alcoholics Anonymous. The programs could have their own steps.

*Non-evidenced-based treatment*[2]: Recovery programs that have no real scientific data indicating success.

*Evidence-based treatment*[3]: Recovery programs that use treatments which have been scientifically proven to help addicts recover from their drug and/or alcohol addiction.

---

1   Chapter 10.
2   Chapter 30.
3   Chapter 30.

## Rehab Background Check

To find potential Rehabs you can use the Internet, but make sure you read Chapter 27 so you will not fall prey to a Rehab's Internet marketing scam. If you have insurance, call the company and get a list of Rehabs they recommend. Check with your government for a list of Rehabs in your state or province. If you are a member of a fellowship group ask members for Rehabs they recommend.

Whatever way you choose to find Rehabs, select several to interview. Be prepared to travel to enter the right Rehab if necessary. Never settle for a potential Toxic Rehab because it is close to you and convenient. This can have bad consequences. Once you have a list of Rehabs, do a background check on each one. The following is how you do that:

- Check the Internet for patient complaints a Rehab might have. Words you can use are "Rehab (name) complaints" and "Rehab (name) fraud." Most Rehabs will have complaints. If a Rehab has complaints, this does not eliminate it from the possibility of using it. What you are looking for is a pattern of the same type of negative comments. If you discover some, you can ask about them during your interview with the Rehab as explained in the next section. If a Rehab has a preponderance of complaints, I would scratch it from your list.

- Search the Internet for government health violations. Use search words like "Rehab (name) Health Violations" and "Rehab (name) Medical Violations." If you find multiple health/medical violations, you have to decide if want to keep the Rehab on your list. This really depends what type of violations they are. If you find violations and decide to keep the Rehab on your list, ask about them during your Rehab Interview.

- Check for Lawsuits/Legal actions filed against the Rehab. Examples of word searches for this include "Rehab (name) law suit," Rehab (name) legal judgements," and Rehab (name) legal cases." If you find any history of multiple lawsuits/legal actions against the Rehab, take it off the list. If you find only one, can keep Rehab on list, but ask questions about it during your Rehab Interview.

## Rehab Interview

The Rehab Interview Check List can be done by phone or in person. Either way you need to be sure you are talking to a person who is qualified to give correct information about the Rehab. Complete the Check List for each Rehab you are thinking about using. Once you get the answers to all 25 questions for each Rehab, you will have to evaluate each answer and decide if one of the Rehabs will work for you. In other words, it will be safe and effective for your recovery.

As mentioned before, even if you are going into a government-sponsored or subsidized Rehab, you should still ask most of the questions on the list. No matter where you go, you still need to be fully informed of your treatment and recovery plan.

## Rehab Interview Check List

1. Is this an Evidence-Based or Non-Evidence-Based Rehab?

    _____

2. Is your recovery program secular or non-secular?

    _____

3. What is your recovery plan, 12 steps or non-12 steps?

    _____

4. How many licensed mental health professionals are on staff?

    _____

5. What kind of training does your staff have, if not licensed?

    _____

6. Will I have one-on-one therapy with a licensed therapist?

    _____

7. Is there a medically supervised detox available if needed?

    _____

8. Is there an intake assessment? If so, who gives it?

    _____

9. Will you discuss my recovery based on my Intake Assessment before I enter Rehab?

   _____

10. What is the average length of stay in Rehab for recovery?

    _____

11. Are family and/or friends involved in my treatment?

    _____

12. After Rehab, will there be any ongoing support for my sobriety?

    _____

13. Are off-label drugs used in Rehab? If so, what are they? On what studies do you base their use?

    _____

14. Is nutrition part of the Rehab program?

    _____

15. Can I get a copy of your Rehab agreement to review before I check in?

    _____

16. Can I receive my medical records soon after my discharge?

    _____

17. Can a person be with me during your Rehab check-in process?

_____

18. What is the phone call and computer-use policy in Rehab?

_____

19. What are the visitation rules in Rehab?

_____

20. If I have food allergies, what are the food options in Rehab?

_____

21. How many years have you been in business?

_____

22. Any questions about your Rehab Back Ground Check, ask now.

_____

23. What are your Rehab Fees and what do they cover? What is your refund policy? Is that policy in writing?

_____

24. Will you accept my insurance for full payment?

_____

25. Will you work with self-pays? If so, is there a payment program? Do you have a discount for self-pays?

---

**A Few Items Before Check In**

Using insurance for payment? Call to see how much they will pay for a Rehab stay and their protocol for billing so you will be informed. You do not want to rely on what the Rehab tells you about your insurance payments. This prevents falling into the same predicament as Survivor did with his insurance billing.

Using a credit card for payment? Then call the card company to find out their dispute policy is on bad services rendered. Ideally you want a card company that will withhold charges until a dispute for bad services is settled between both parties. Unfortunately, Survivor's card company did not do this. Which caused him months of doubts and stress going back and forth with the card company.

Survivor did check with his other card's billing policies later to see if there was a difference in dispute procedures. He discovered some would have automatically refunded him in the first dispute, some would not. The ones that would have automatically refunded him, would had shifted the burden of proof to the Rehab for the questionable billing, not him. It will save you a big headache if you can use a card company that you know ahead of time will be on your side if you receive Toxic Rehab services.

Enlist a loved one or friend to go with and be at your side during your entire check-in process at the Rehab. Do not let the

Rehab separate you from this person before you enter the Rehab, or it could be the start of a Toxic Rehab stay.

## Rehab's Intake Assessment

Here are 15 typical questions that should be included in all Intake Assessments in every Rehab worldwide. These questions and your answers insure that you receive a correct diagnosis and treatment recovery plan. Questions might not be in the order as given and the list certainly is not all inclusive. The questions give you a good idea what is needed for a professional intake assessment. The person giving the assessment and analyzing the results should be licensed and specialize in the process. You do not want the assessment given by a salesperson or untrained person. The 15 sample questions are:

1. Age, gender, marital or partner status, and educational status?
2. Occupation and financial status?
3. Culture and ethnicity background?
4. Complete medical history?
5. Taking any medications? If so, what are they for?
6. Psychiatric/psychological history?
7. History of addiction and what type of drugs?
8. Patients insight to your addiction?
9. Any previous recovery treatment? If so, what happened?
10. Motivation for recovery?
11. Any need for additional medical or financial support?
12. Religious preference?

13. Patient's perceived strengths and weaknesses?
14. What drug(s) last used, and how much?
15. Relationship status with spouse, parents, siblings, partners, friends?

The only thing I would like to add to this. If you are receiving an Intake Assessment from a professional, be as honest as you can be with the answers. It will make a big difference in your recovery treatment plan.

# R.N.'S AFFIDAVIT

Affidavit of Natalie ~~Shryne~~

I, Natalie, have looked at the following described documentation from the Rehab in connection with the patient's stay at the facility. I have made observations on each document.

## 1. Doctor's orders/plan for patient's rehab stay

- Observations: States patient has a withdrawal score of 1 and a pain score of 0 out of 10. Assessment will be continued and patient monitored every two hours. Patient is referred to as a male several times, then as a female. In other reports I have viewed, the patient is also referred to as male sometimes, then female.

## 2. Nursing charts for checking/watching patient during his stay

- Observations: 4 charts reflect 4 nights of checking on patient. Only one chart for the first night stay reflects patient was actually checked at 03:30 and his vitals checked. The rest of the charts state patient was asleep and was not checked or vitals taken during the night.

- Chart for start of the 2nd night of patient's stay shows he went to bed at 22:25. The chart for the morning of the third day of patients stays shows he was not awoken at any time for vitals to be checked. It just states at 02:25 patient appears to be asleep.

## 3. Three separate lab reports and ECG report on patient

- Observation: All three lab reports state gender not supplied or physician name by rehab. Since no gender supplied, therefore lab reports state adult female references ranges were applied.

- One test shows negative for acetaminophen.

- ECG shows an unconfirmed analysis.

## 4. Documents with patient's intake and discharge days

- Observation: Document shows patient entered rehab one afternoon, stayed that night, and the subsequent three nights. Then he was discharged at 9 am the morning of the fourth night.

## 5. Patient's drug screen results

- Observation: Of all the drugs listed that were tested, patient shows positive for only one, Benzodiazepines.

## 6. Patient's request to Rehab for all his personal medical files

- Observation: Patient requests all his medical files to be released only to him, nobody else. What he signed reflects this request.

## 7. Letter from Rehab's attorney to patient about his personal medical files

- Observation: Rehab sent patient's medical files to their attorney, and letter states attorney has patient's medical files and is sending patients records to him, minus any documentation/records he [the attorney] deems belongs his client [Rehab].

Page 1 of 2

**8. Patient's medication administration record**

- Observation: The day after patient checked in, his chart shows he is given Trileptal and Neurontin. The chart reflects the next day he refused to take either drug.

**9. Various nursing assessment reports taken the day patient checked into detox**

- Observation: Overall mental/physical health excellent. Appearance, memory, speech, reflexes good.

**10. Report assessment by doctor on patient 24 hours into his stay**

- Observation: Report states patient's withdrawal risk score was at 0.

**11. Assessment report by a doctor**

- Observation: Report states patient was using Valium (10 mg, one a day on and off) for a few months.

**12. Various paperwork on the morning of patient's discharge**

- Observation: Report by a doctor states patient had no post-withdrawal symptomatology and had no apparent withdrawal symptoms. Doctor wants patient to take Trileptal for 9 more days. I see the prescription the doctor wrote for Trileptal.

**13. The Rehabs enhanced-recovery service document**

- Observation: This document states the Rehab has Reiki, Hypnotherapy, Yoga, Chi Kung, etc.

**14. Rehab document**

- Observation: Document states if you file a complaint against the Rehab, they will not penalize you.

**15. Rehab agreement for patient's stay**

- Observation: Documents states 7 days of detox for a charge of $1000.00 for each day.

**16. Letter to from State Bar to patient**

- Observation: Letter has a case number in it.

_Natalee_ _____ R. N. 6-15-18

Natalie _____ R. N.

# GLOSSARY

**Abstinence:** Refraining from further drug use

**Addiction Assessment:** A way to determine the presence and severity of chemical dependency in a person

**Addiction Treatment:** Program to reduce addiction

**Addiction:** Ongoing activity that continuously causes harm to oneself or others

**Addictive Personality:** Trait(s) that develop in response to drug use

**Age at Onset:** Age at which one's addictive behavior began.

**Antagonist:** Drug(s) that can nullify another drugs effects

**AOD:** Alcohol and Other Drugs

**AODA:** Alcohol and Other Drug Abuse

**Blood Alcohol Level/Concentration:** Concentration level of alcohol in the bloodstream

**Central Nervous System (CNS):** Brain and spinal cord

**Clinical Opiate Withdrawal Scale (COWS):** Used to determine the severity of opioid withdrawal

**Cold Turkey:** Instantly stopping using alcohol and/or a drug

**Coping Strategies:** Strategies that people use to cope with life

**D.O.C.:** Drug of Choice

**Delirium Tremens (DTs):** Extreme withdrawal symptoms experienced when a person stops the use of alcohol and/or drugs

**Denial:** Failure to accept there is an addiction

**Detoxification (Detox):** The process of the body removing alcohol and/or drugs from the body

**Drug Tolerance:** Decreased responsiveness to a drug

**Dual Diagnosis:** A person has mental health issues in addition to addiction

**Ethanol:** Alcoholic beverage

**Evidence-based Treatment:** Scientifically validated treatment approaches

**Maintenance:** Stabilization of a patient who is indefinitely on a drug's lowest effective dose

**Negative Reinforcement:** Repetitive behavior to avoid something unpleasant

**Off-Label Use:** Physician-approved use of a drug for uses other than those stated on its label

# Glossary

**Opioid Agonist:** Activates opioid receptors in the brain

**Opioid Antagonist:** Blocks opioid agonist effects

**Over-the-Counter Drugs:** Legal non-prescription drugs

**Post-Acute Withdrawal Syndrome (PAWS):** Long term withdrawal symptoms

**Relapse Triggers:** Events that can lead people back into addiction

**Relapse:** Symptom recurrence after a period of sobriety or drug-use cessation

**Remission:** A symptom-free period

**Reversed Tolerance:** When a lower dose of a drug produces the same effect that previously resulted with a higher dosage

**Side Effects:** Secondary effects of a drug that are negative.

**Tapering Off:** Slowly reducing the dosage over time so that the body has a chance to adjust. If the process is followed carefully enough, the individual might experience few if any withdrawal symptoms

**Tolerance:** Condition in which one must increase the use of a drug for it to have the same effect

**Toxicity:** Degree of poisonousness

**Trigger:** Circumstance that results in an addiction relapse

# INDEX

# Index

# Index

# Index

**U**
van Mierlo, Dr. Trevor, 81

**V**
vitamins/minerals, 101, 103–104, 107,
    195

**W**
Wilson, William Griffith, 132
withdrawal, 88, 103, 119–122, 124,
    163, 183, 208–209
Women for Sobriety (WFS), 19, 51–54
    acceptance statements, 52–53
    elements for change, 52
    group meetings, 53–54
    member insights, 55–56
    overview, 51–54

## ABOUT THE AUTHORS

 **Steve Murray** is the author of 12 self-help books. He also has a series of 25 self-healing programs on DVD. The DVD topics include: Cancer Guided Imagery, weight loss, pain relief, fear and stress relief, and Reiki Attunements, just to name a few. Steve is married with a son and lives in Las Vegas, NV.

 **Survivor** is a retired Real Estate Investor with three adult kids and five grandkids. He lives with his wife and German Shepherd in Las Vegas, NV. When not spoiling his grandkids, he plays golf as much as possible.

# Notes

# Notes